POWERHOUSE
HANDS

POWERHOUSE
HANDS

How to Recognize
and
Get the Most
from
Your Big Cards

by Albert Dormer

PRENTICE-HALL, INC., Englewood Cliffs, N.J.

Powerhouse Hands: How to Recognize
and Get the Most from Your Big Cards
by Albert Dormer
Copyright © 1975 by Albert Dormer

Printed in the United States of America

Prentice-Hall International, Inc., London
Prentice-Hall of Australia, Pty. Ltd., Sydney
Prentice-Hall of Canada, Ltd., Toronto
Prentice-Hall of India Private Ltd., New Delhi
Prentice-Hall of Japan, Inc., Tokyo

10 9 8 7 6 5 4 3 2 1

Library of Congress Cataloging in Publication Data

Dormer, Albert.
  Powerhouse hands.

  1. Contract bridge. I. Title.
GV1282.3.D57   795.4'152   75-4700
ISBN 0-13-686667-0
ISBN 0-13-686659-X pbk.

Introduction

Albert Dormer is the most rewarding "find" I ever made via mail order. Knowing him only by reputation and through his writings, I succeeded in luring him to the United States to become associate editor of the *Contract Bridge Bulletin*, by far the world's most widely circulated bridge magazine.

To the great regret of all who knew him and his work here, Dormer later elected to return to his native England. But he has continued prominent in the American bridge scene as a valued member of the Goren Editorial Board and a contributing editor to the *Official Encyclopedia of Bridge*. He has also played a leading role in analyzing the bids and plays in the American Contract Bridge League's annual book on the world bridge championships.

Dormer is the author of some of the better contributions not only in American bridge magazines but in others all over the world. He has co-authored no fewer than seven books with Britain's top bridge writer, Terence Reese, and he has contributed substantially to others.

Before he put aside the shuffle and deal and took up a busy pen, Dormer was a highly successful tournament player, among other achievements having twice won the Gold Cup, Britain's premier event. Now he has decided to take a vacation from writing books and return to the card table, where you may expect him once again to prove that it will be profitable to do not only as he says but as he does. Meanwhile, however, he continues his editorship of "World Bridge News," the official medium of the World Bridge Federation, and his other journalistic activities.

Through this book you will have a delightful opportunity to join the growing group of Dormer devotees. Also, to improve your successes with powerhouse hands

—Richard L. Frey

Preface

There are so many books on bridge that a writer who ventures to add to the number had better have a good reason for doing so. When I was invited to contribute a volume on powerhouse hands to the Prentice-Hall Contract Bridge Series, my first reaction was to question whether the existing coverage of this subject left any · room for useful addition. However, having learned over the years to respect Richard Frey's unerring judgment in all matters concerning authorship and the modern bridge scene, and especially the two together, I agreed to think it over.

I found to my surprise that there is not at the present time any book addressed wholly to this important subject, and that treatment of the subject in comprehensive bridge books tends to be distinctly sketchy. I therefore accepted Editor Frey's assignment, and in fulfilling it I have experienced considerable satisfaction, which I hope will be shared by the reader.

After all, powerhouse hands do not come along very often—at least for your side. When they do, I hope the advice in this book will ensure that you gain maximum profit from them.

In general, I have aimed to describe the best modern methods used by players from average to expert level. If some meritorious practices are not mentioned, this is not out of lack of respect for them, but from the necessity of keeping to a reasonable length.

—Albert Dormer

Contents

POWERHOUSE
HANDS

1

Winner or Loser?

♠ ♡ ◇ ♣

Powerhouse Hands Make
the Difference

When you find you have stopped in game with a hand that belongs in slam, do you seek consolation in the bromide that tells you it's never wrong to settle for a sure profit? If so, you should ask yourself this question: If you don't bid your cold slams, and the opponents do bid their cold slams, where is the sure profit?

To be a successful bridge player your bidding must be forceful and accurate enough to allow you to win *big* on big hands. This is simply a reflection of the way bridge is scored. It explains why in the international arena experts have been compelled by Italy's example to recognize that they must revise their methods, paying much more attention to big hands. The purpose of this book is to enable you, too, to follow this example by a more vigorous and logical use of standard methods aided by modern conventions.

Most powerhouse hands fall into one of four categories:

1. The **huge** single hand that can virtually go it alone as far as game.

♠ A K Q J 10 3   ♡ A K 10   ◇ —   ♣ A Q 9 4

Everybody can recognize this hand as a powerhouse: When you pick it up you feel that now, for once, you are the master of your fate. All the same, the magic ingredient is the paltry strength in the right places needed across the table to enable this hand to become still more powerful.

PLAYERS WHO LOSE in this kind of hand do so because they fail to spark partner into life when his anemic holdings happen to be just what are needed. Or they are so carried away with their own hand that they overbid despite partner's despairing wave of a red flag.

    2. The **combined** balanced powerhouse where the partners together have 33 or more of the high-card points.

      ♠ K Q 6   ♡ A Q 8 2   ◇ A Q 4   ♣ A K J

This type is the easiest to handle: All you have to do is tell partner how many points you've got—or have partner tell you how many points he has. PLAYERS WHO LOSE are those who fail to communicate the needed information, usually because at some point in the auction they make an imprecise bid in a suit when it would have been better to select a bid in notrump, defining their point count.

    3. The **big** trump fit where an abundance of trumps in each hand plus suitable distributional features will greatly exalt the high-card strength of the two hands.

    ♠ A 10 8 5 3 2   ♡ —   ◇ A Q 10 7 3   ♣ K 4

If you have this hand and are fortunate enough to learn that your partner has strong support for either spades or diamonds, you must be able to judge how enormous your hand has become, and you must know how to communicate this to your partner so that he too will be sufficiently ambitious. PLAYERS WHO LOSE are those who fail to convince partner that a big trump fit is present and that only key cards are important; or who fail to locate the vital controls needed to exploit the fit.

    4. The **delicate** "fitters," which may or may not belong at a trump contract. These are the numerous hands where better-than-

average holdings by both players may become still greater through the tonic of a perfect fit—or where superficial strength may be eroded because no fit is present.

♠ A 4   ♡ K 10 2   ◊ A Q 9 5 2   ♣ K Q 3

    Here you may make a slam with no more than 28 or 29 points if partner can help your diamonds, and especially if he too has a five-card suit which you can help. This type hand calls for gentle exploratory bidding. PLAYERS WHO LOSE are those who make a stultifying bid in notrump when it would have been better to bid a suit, and who thus fail to discover how well the hands combine. Or they fail to realize that what sounds like strong bidding from both sides of the table is drained of power because there is no fit.

    If you have recognized here some of the reasons why you are not getting the best out of your powerhouse hands, you will be anxious to learn what you can do about it. Later we will look at the best modern techniques, which will enable you to give these hands the VIP treatment they deserve. But in the remainder of this chapter I should like to dwell upon certain fundamentals that apply throughout the bidding process.

VALUING YOUR HAND

    What addition should be made to the familiar 4-3-2-1 count (A-K-Q-J) to allow for the extra value of long suits? Several methods are in common use, all based on the idea of reaching game with 26 points (though 25 points in high cards are enough for 3 NT, and you need 29 for game in a minor). All, too, are based on reaching a slam with 33 or 34, and a grand slam with 37.

    The points needed for each bid in the auction are the same no matter which method you favor. If you have a liking for your present method of counting distributional points, which perhaps is the very popular method of adding 3 points for a void, 2 for a singleton and 1 for a doubleton, you should certainly stay with it. Personally, I am impressed by the argument that the real distributional values in a hand consist of *long* suits, not short suits, and I therefore like to add points for length, as follows:

> *Add 1 point for the fifth card in any suit.*
> *Add 1 point for the sixth card in any suit.*
> *Add 2 points for each subsequent card.*

In many hands this comes to the same as adding 3-2-1 for shortness. (When you have a long suit, you must have a corresponding shortage.) Sometimes it reduces your count a little, as when you have no real length. But sometimes it enhances it, as here:

♠ A J 10 9 4 3 2   ♡ A J   ◇ 8 3   ♣ A Q

If you add 1 point for each doubleton, this hand contains only 3 distributional points, making the hand worth 19 points in all. In the long-suit method the suit is more accurately valued at 4 points.

Shortness itself is no advantage unless you have a trump fit with your partner. Then, of course, it is extremely important to add still more points to reflect such valuable features as singletons, voids and doubletons. This is a more skilful process than is generally admitted, and is covered fully in Chapter 4.

ASSESSING THE FIT

Chico Marx was playing with Ivan Erdos in a TV bridge series, all three now deceased, alas. Chico bid his head off. Then, noting Ivan's dazed expression on first sight of dummy, he said defensively, "In Hollywood, that's a good hand." His partner was constrained to point out that no man is an island and that a vital test of a powerhouse hand is how well it fits in with partner. (On that occasion, singularly badly!)

As the purpose of bidding is to assess the value of two hands *in combination*, you should always ask yourself the meaning of partner's bids and try to visualize his hand. Consider this sequence:

	PARTNER	YOU
	1 ♡	2 ♠
	3 ♣	3 ♠
	3 NT	?

You hold:

♠ A Q 9 7 6 3   ♡ A   ◇ A K J   ♣ 7 5 4

If, as the bidding develops, you have begun to view this hand with steadily mounting concern, you are well ahead. Readers who despite its apparent promise are beginning to doubt whether it really has any future beyond game are not doing badly; those who still have their sights set firmly on a slam have everything to learn.

Opener has bid two suits and can hardly have less than Q-x-x in the unbid suit, diamonds. He is therefore apt to be very short on spades, and this hurts your hand. Partner cannot have great compensating strength as he is evidently willing to settle for game despite your force. As the hands appear to fit so poorly, responder should be concerned only to find the safest game contract. In fact, it would be unwise even to go beyond 3 NT, as the two hands may well be as follows:

PARTNER		YOU	
♠	4	♠	A Q 9 7 6 3
♡	K Q J 8 3	♡	A
◇	Q 10 7	◇	A K J
♣	K J 9 2	♣	7 5 4

Any further move may lead to a minus score.

The next example shows the other side of the coin: Responder learns as the bidding progresses that the fit is enormous.

OPENER	RESPONDER
1 ♠	2 ♠
3 ◇	4 ♠
5 ◇	?

Responder holds:

♠ K 7 4 3 2   ♡ 9 7 4   ◇ K 5   ♣ 10 6 4

There is only one logical explanation of opener's bidding. He is saying: "Despite your weak initial response, a slam is still possible. I have spades and diamonds and diamonds and spades. I am interested only in your holdings in these two suits." As responder could not conceivably be better equipped in these suits (within the limits set by his 2 ♠ bid), he should bid 6 ♠! Opener's hand must be something like this:

♠ A Q 10 8 5   ♡ A 8 2   ◇ A Q 9 7 3   ♣ —

THE PRINCIPLE OF THE LIMIT BID

In general it is good style to use as few bids as possible. When you can "limit" your hand by describing its strength and character in one bid, this is better than employing a whole series of bids.

♠ Q J 9 3   ♡ K J 4   ◇ K J 8 5   ♣ A Q

If it is your habit to open 1 ◇ or 1 ♠ rather than 1 NT with this type of hand, it may be that you are not fully seized of the principle of the limit bid. One advantage accrues when there is intervention: Here, if you open 1 NT and there is any kind of overcall, your partner will be well able to take suitable action as he knows your hand within fairly close limits. Suppose instead that you open with 1 ◇ and there is an overcall of 2 ♣. All kinds of uncertainties may now arise, leading quite possibly to gnashing of teeth and beating of breasts. (How many points does the responder need now for a free bid? If your partner passes and you reopen, what precise strength is shown by later bids? And so on.)

Even with a clear run there is no guarantee that if you open at one of a suit you will reach a better contract than a player who limits his hand by opening 1 NT. After 1 ◇ -1 ♡ -1 ♠, for example, your partner still cannot be sure how strong you are (you could be anywhere in the 13-19 point range) nor does he know that you have a club guard.

When there is one bid that limits your hand, you should usually choose this bid. Suppose that your partner opens 1 ♡, next hand passes and you hold:

♠ 6   ♡ K J 9 3 2   ◇ 10 5   ♣ K J 7 6 4

Go straight to 4 ♡. To bid 2 ♣ as an introductory move is a poor strategy, as the opponents may be able to bid spades or diamonds. Or the bidding may develop in such a way that you are never able to show just how enormous your heart support is.

The theory of the limit bid is that *the partner* of the player who makes this bid will often be able to head straight for the best spot. In the following deal from an international team trial the opener was able to select an excellent contract because his partner made an intelligent limit bid.

OPENER	RESPONDER
♠ A K J 10 3 2	♠ 9
♡ Q 5	♡ A K J 10 8 6 4
◇ A 5 3 2	◇ 6
♣ K	♣ Q 9 8 3

OPENER	RESPONDER
1 ♠	4 ♡ (!)
4 NT	5 ◇
6 ♡	Pass

The key, of course, was the responder's very first bid. This player was Jeremy Flint, then little known, who subsequently became a world champion contender and leading theorist. Flint quite reasonably decided that he wanted to be in 4 ♡ opposite any kind of opening hand—so he bid 4 ♡. Now his partner found it easy to reckon that a contract of 6 ♡ would depend at worst on a finesse. (That, incidentally, is a good test of whether a small slam is mathematically worth bidding.)

At other tables the responder bid only 2 ♡, which no doubt is the bid that most players would make. The opener's next bid was a strength-showing 3 ♠, and now the responder found himself with no good move to make. A Blackwood bid of 4 NT would not have helped, for after a response of 5 ♡ it would not have been clear how many club losers there were in the hand. In actual play the bidding at most tables petered out in this sequence:

OPENER	RESPONDER
1 ♠	2 ♡
3 ♠	4 ♡
Pass	

The principle, then, is that you should look not just for a bid, but for one that will express the full strength of your hand. Head straight for the best contract when it is visible, and be scientific only when you must. *You* may know exactly what you mean when you open in one suit, "reverse" into another and later make an inferential cue bid in a third suit. What counts, however, is whether your partner knows too.

A player should always be conscious of whether he has or has not succeeded in limiting his hand. One of the deadly sins of bridge is committed when a player who has made a limit bid fails to respect a decision by his partner based on that bid.

OPENER	RESPONDER
1 ♡	1 ♠
3 ♡	4 ♡
?	

Opener holds:

♠ Q 7   ♡ K J 9 7 5 2   ◇ A 10 4   ♣ A K

There are still players at large who do not appreciate that opener, having limited his hand with a 3 ♡ rebid that shows 17 to 19 points and a six-card suit, must pass automatically when his partner merely bids game. Responder may have scraped up his raise to 4 ♡ on a wing and a prayer. If opener were to make any further bid now, this would lead to the absurd situation where the hand could be played in 3 ♡ or 5 ♡ (or 6 ♡) but never 4 ♡! Opener may think: "I have a maximum hand, 19 points, with excellent controls and a high card in partner's spade suit. Now that my rather ragged heart suit has been supported, I am going to have a shot at slam." This is folly, of course, for these values have already been shown.

By limiting your hand early you may often avoid altogether a problem that would be quite unnerving. Consider this hand from a previous page, where partner opens 1 ♡ and you hold:

♠ 6   ♡ K J 9 3 2   ◇ 10 5   ♣ K J 7 6 4

Suppose, first, that you raise straight to 4 ♡ in approved fashion. Whatever happens now, you are home free. If fourth hand bids

4 ♠ and your partner doubles, this is no problem; you may take your stand by the Tennysonian principle that simple faith is more than Norman blood. Partner knows what kind of hand you have, and you don't know what kind of hand he has, so you pass the double with a virtuous glow.

Now suppose, instead, that the bidding goes:

PARTNER	OPPONENT	YOU	OPPONENT
1 ♡	Pass	2 ♣	4 ♠
Double	Pass	?	

This time you are most unhappy—or should be. As you have not yet supported your partner's suit, you are more or less obligated to bid 5 ♡. But if it turns out that this contract cannot be made and that 4 ♠ would have been defeated, the best you can do now is to admit, "*Mea culpa.*"

DEVELOPING YOUR JUDGMENT

A bridge book can do little more than describe the main framework of bidding. When this has been mastered you must aim to fill in the gaps from your own experience.

Many of the finer points are well-known: a holding such as K-x or A-Q in a suit that has been bid on your right is worth more than face value, and so on. The process of refinement can go much further, as this example shows:

PARTNER	YOU
1 ♠	2 ♡
4 ♡	?

You hold:

♠ 6 2   ♡ A J 9 8 4   ◇ 10 6 3   ♣ A K 5

Do you pass 4 ♡ or press on toward slam by cue-bidding ♣ A? This is a very close decision, and no one could say you were wrong either way. However, the particular question that I want to ask is, how do you rate your holding in spades? Because your partner has opened with this suit, you would of course have looked with favor on the presence of a high honor card. As it is, would you say that your actual holding in spades is better or worse than, say, three small cards? Or a singleton?

Well, my proposition is that for slam purposes a small doubleton is not at all a bad holding in a suit where partner is expected to hold considerable strength. Such a holding combines good chances for the profitable development of the suit with good prospects of keeping the unavoidable losers within bounds. Let's look at some of the likely spade holdings that your partner may have in this particular bidding sequence.

(1) ♠ A K 8 7 4
(2) ♠ K Q 7 5 3
(3) ♠ A Q J 4 3

A study of these examples shows that when developing this side suit you are likely to do better with a holding of two small cards in your hand than with a holding of either three cards or one. The thinking player permits such matters to sway a close decision, and in that way he develops good judgment. In the example above, this consideration should persuade you to bid 5 ♣.

Some players make no attempt to take into account any hand but their own, and it can be very frustrating to play with such an unimaginative partner. Suppose you open 3 ♠, vulnerable, and your partner responds with 3 NT. You hold:

♠ K Q J 8 7 6 4   ♡ 2   ◇ 10 8 7   ♣ 9 6

The right move, of course, is to pass. You have said your piece and it is to be presumed that your partner either feels sure of bringing in the spade suit or has a long, solid minor suit, with protection in the other suits. However, unless you have led a very sheltered life you have probably encountered the type of responder who, opposite an opening bid of 3 ♠, bids 3 NT with this type of hand:

♠ —   ♡ A J 8 4   ♢ A K 9 6 3   ♣ A Q 8 4

With this hand the unimaginative player may think: "Partner has a long spade suit and I have 18 points, with the other suits wrapped up. I am going to bid 3 NT." This is an atrocity, of course—the correct bid is 4 ♠. Responder has only to try to visualize any typical 3 ♠ hand in combination with his own to see that although 4 ♠ is not certain to make, a contract of 3 NT is certain *not* to make.

Imagination is especially necessary when one player has a powerhouse hand and the other holds small treasures. When your partner bids up to the skies and you have Q-x-x in his first suit and K-x in his second suit, you should reach for your rose-colored spectacles. Equally, when you can see that your values may be largely wasted, you should be cautious.

Imagination, however, is a two-edged weapon. (If you question this, think back to what some of your partners have done to you lately—or vice versa!) Your partner may choose the same moment to exert *his* powers of imagination too, leading to overheating. Be disciplined, therefore, until the later rounds of bidding. When you are confident that your next bid will put an end to matters, you may decide to take a position. But do not make fancy bids early in the auction. And especially, do not overstate your values early. It is often possible to correct a slight underbid, but there is no way of telling partner, later, that you do not have the values you said you had.

THE USE OF CONVENTIONAL BIDS

There are too many conventions in modern bridge. This assertion may raise a hollow laugh from the reader who, having glanced through the contents of this book, has observed the presence of such items as the Flint Convention, Jacoby Transfers and Key-card Blackwood. Nevertheless, I have noticed that, although the quest for increased efficiency is unabated, many experts have begun to discard some of their less productive conventions rather than take new ones on board.

When you read about a new convention, remember that *you* are the best judge of whether this convention will really help your game. Does the convention appear so logical *to you* that you will easily remember how it works? Even the very best players will not adopt a new convention unless they are sure that the technical advantage outweighs the memory strain.

Use sparingly the conventions that you do adopt. Remember that each time you make a conventional bid you give information to the opponents as well as to your partner. It is obviously a poor idea to do so if this information is useless to your partner and, at the same time, useful to your opponents. Do not, therefore, bid a Blackwood 4 NT, or 2 ♣ over 1 NT or use any other conventional bid, unnecessarily. Many a contract has been broken, just because those words were spoken. This hand occurred in match play:

```
                    NORTH
                    ♠ K J 9 8 2
                    ♡ 8 4
                    ◇ 6 3
                    ♣ A J 8 5
WEST                                    EAST
♠ 7 4                                   ♠ 5
♡ K 7 3 2                               ♡ 9 6 5
◇ 8 4 2                                 ◇ K Q 10 7 5
♣ Q 10 9 7                              ♣ K 6 4 2
                    SOUTH
                    ♠ A Q 10 6 3
                    ♡ A Q J 10
                    ◇ A J 9
                    ♣ 3
```

SOUTH	WEST	NORTH	EAST
1 ♠	Pass	4 ♠	Pass
4 NT	Pass	5 ◇	Dble
6 ♠	Pass	Pass	Pass

When this deal was played, West led a diamond in response to his partner's double, forcing out declarer's ace. Declarer drew trumps and took the heart finesse but this failed and West returned a diamond to defeat the contract.

The slam was a reasonable contract but it would have held better prospects if South had not wheeled out the Blackwood Convention. After the raise to 4 ♠, South could see that he wanted to be in 6 ♠—and no more than 6 ♠—whether his partner held one ace or none. South should therefore have bid 6 ♠ direct. West *might* still have found the killing diamond lead, but if he did not the slam would have been made, a diamond from dummy going away on a heart.

A game of bridge is full of mistakes like these, waiting to trap the unprepared. If you can avoid error on most of your powerhouse hands, you will be well on the way to becoming a better player.

2

Powerhouse Openings

♠   ♡   ◇   ♣

The Artificial 2 ♣ Opening—The Response to 2 ♣—Opener's Rebid After 2 ♣—Responder's Rebid After 2 ♣—Ace Responses to 2 ♣ ("CAB")—4 NT After 2 ♣—The Forcing 2-Bid—Intermediate (Acol) 2-Bids—Other Strong Openings

Sometimes even you will be fortunate enough to pick up a hand that is strong enough to produce game all by itself. To open with a direct bid of game on such a hand would practically destroy all chance of reaching a slam, and therefore the universal practice is to open with a forcing bid, so that the feast of reason and flow of soul may continue until the best contract is reached.

For many years most players used the happy-go-lucky method of the Forcing 2-bid: The openings of 2 ♣, 2 ◇, 2 ♡ and 2 ♠ were all treated as game-forcing bids based on a giant hand and a genuine suit. However, with the general drive for improvement, many staunch supporters of the Forcing 2-bid have been forced to admit that it hardly makes sense to reserve all these bids for one very powerful type of hand that occurs infrequently. In modern "Standard," therefore, an increasing number of players, including nearly all tournament players, open 2 ♣ on all hands that were formerly opened with a Forcing 2-bid.

There are so many benefits to this procedure that any player still wedded to the old-style Forcing 2-bid may confidently expect to

improve his game several notches by switching to the modern 2 ♣
opening. The Forcing 2-bid is fully covered later in this chapter, and
the author admits that in point of popularity it should come first. But
he is hoping that many devotees of this bid will throw off the
comfortable old chains and subscribe to the more efficient method.

The Artificial 2 ♣ Opening

In the modern style of bidding there is only one opening that
announces a powerhouse hand and, with the exception of two
specialized sequences, insists on the bidding being kept open until
game is reached. This is an opening bid of 2 ♣.

The 2 ♣ bid is artificial in that it bears no relation at all to the
club suit. But the fact that you do not show a genuine suit until the
second round does not mean that the 2 ♣ opening is wasteful and
uneconomical. In most cases, opener and responder can say much
more about their hands while still at the two level than with the
old-style Forcing 2-bid. Moreover, by using just one bid to cover all
game-going openings regardless of opener's real suit, the other
2-bids can be used either as preemptive Weak 2-bids, a very popular
method, or to show powerful distributional hands that may produce
a lot of tricks if the responder has one or two cards in the right
places. The choice is yours; but you have that choice only if you use
2 ♣ to cover all game-forcing hands.*

THE REQUIREMENTS FOR 2 ♣

Two types of hand qualify for an opening bid of 2 ♣:
1) Any hand containing 23 or more high-card points.
2) Any powerful distributional hand that offers a reasonable
likelihood of game, even though it may contain somewhat less than
23 points. This type of hand should normally include at least five
honor tricks.

*But see artificial 1 ♣ openings, Chapter 10.

The following hands all qualify for an opening bid of 2 ♣:

(1) ♠ A K J 10 7 5 3   ♡ A   ◇ A Q 8   ♣ K 4
(2) ♠ A Q 7   ♡ K Q 10 7 5   ◇ A   ♣ A K Q 4
(3) ♠ A K J 7   ♡ A Q 8   ◇ A J 5   ♣ K Q 7

Hand (1) is an obvious game-forcing type where, although you have "only" 21 high-card points, you are willing to take your chance in a contract of 4 ♠ as long as partner has thirteen cards. The hand is far too strong for a direct opening of 4 ♠, and that itself is proof that the hand qualifies for 2 ♣.

Hand (2) is of a type where the likely final contract is uncertain: You may wind up in hearts, clubs or notrump, or in spades if partner has this suit. To open 2 ♣ and bid hearts on the next round at least establishes a forcing situation and allows time for investigation.

The method of dealing with the third type of hand requires some elaboration. It was mentioned earlier that the 2 ♣ opening bid is forcing to game with the exception of two subsequent sequences. One such sequence is as follows:

OPENER	RESPONDER
2 ♣	2 ◇
2 NT	

Here the opener is saying: "I have 23 or 24 points in a balanced hand. You may pass if your hand is worthless." If the responder makes *any* further bid, however, the situation again becomes game-forcing.

With Hand (3), therefore, which contains 24 points, you open with 2 ♣, intending to rebid in notrump at the minimum level over any response. (With a similar type of balanced hand, containing 25 or 26 points, you would open 2 ♣ and rebid 3 NT.)

Note that the 2 ♣ opening followed by a 2 NT rebid is a most

valuable sequence and should therefore be used with some flexibil
ity. Suppose you have this hand:

♠ A K Q 10 3   ♥ K 4   ♦ K J 2   ♣ A Q 8

You need awfully little from partner, but the hand is not quite
strong enough for a 2 ♣ opening and a 2 ♠ rebid, which would
commit you to game opposite little better than a bust. As the fifth
card in the nearly solid spade suit is worth an extra point, you should
treat this as a 23-point hand and open 2 ♣, to be followed not by
2 ♠ but by 2 NT.

Here are two types of hand that do not qualify for 2 ♣:

(4) ♠ 2   ♥ A K J 9 8 4 3   ♦ Q 2   ♣ K Q J
(5) ♠ A 8 7 6 3   ♥ A K   ♦ K Q J   ♣ A J 8

With the first example you certainly hope to make a game, but
the hand lacks the high-card strength for 2 ♣. Therefore the recommended opening is 1 ♥; or perhaps, in third or fourth position,
4 ♥.

Hand (5) also is not strong enough for 2 ♣. The poor quality
of the long suit and the inflexible honors in the red suits, which are
unaccompanied by small cards, combine to suggest that 2 NT is the
correct opening. This call, as we shall now see, has been adjusted in
strength because of the advent of the 2 ♣ opening.

EFFECT ON THE 2 NT AND 3 NT OPENINGS

As balanced hands of 23-24 points can be shown by opening
2 ♣ and rebidding 2 NT, a direct opening bid of 2 NT now shows
21 or 22, or perhaps an exceptionally "good" 20 points.

With the 3 NT opening, too, the old idea of using this to show
a very strong balanced hand of 25-27 points is abandoned, as such a
hand can be shown by opening 2 ♣ and rebidding 3 NT. Many
tournament players now play the "Gambling" 3 NT, an attractive
convention but one that can be safely recommended only to those

with fairly strong nerves. The idea is that you open 3 NT with a long, solid minor suit and little or nothing outside.

♠ 9 2   ♡ 6   ◇ 10 7 4   ♣ A K Q J 8 3 2

Devotees of the Gambling 3 NT would open 3 NT with this hand at any vulnerability! The responding hand is now in complete control. He may take out into 4 ♣ (which the opener would convert to 4 ◇ if that were his real suit). Or he may decide to stand firm; in this case opener must do the same, even if doubled. Used in this way, the Gambling 3 NT has the merit of a high-level preempt while not foregoing the possibility of playing in 3 NT.

Quiz on the 2 ♣ Opening

What is your opening bid on each of the following hands?

(1) ♠ A 4 ♡ A K Q J 7 5 ◇ A K J ♣ 10 5
(2) ♠ A Q 6 4 3 ♡ K Q 8 ◇ A 4 2 ♣ A K
(3) ♠ A Q 3 ♡ 7 ◇ A K J 4 2 ♣ A K 6 3
(4) ♠ A K Q 4 ♡ K Q 3 ◇ A Q J ♣ A J 2
(5) ♠ A J 10 9 3 ♡ A K Q 10 ◇ 7 ♣ A K 10

Solutions

1. 2 ♣. In general, you should be unwilling to stay out of game with any hand where you need to find partner with only one of several holdings to be sure of your contract. Here, if partner has ◇ Q, ♠ K or ♣ A, you have ten almost certain tricks, with the additional possibility of finding him with a doubleton diamond. You therefore open 2 ♣ and rebid hearts.

2. 2 NT. This shows 21 or 22 points. To open 2 ♣ and rebid

2 NT would suggest 23 or 24 points, and this hand does not warrant such treatment.

3. 1 ◇. If you held the same hand with 5-4 in the major suits you might just about open 2 ♣, but as it is it would be unwise to insist on game. In fact, if partner is unable to respond to an opening bid of 1 ◇, it is unlikely that you can make a game. You should therefore content yourself with a modest opening bid, hoping that partner will be able to cooperate. By and large, whenever you are in doubt that your hand is worth a 2 ♣ opening—it isn't.

4. 2 ♣. Balanced hands containing 25 or 26 points are shown by opening 2 ♣ and rebidding 3 NT.

5. 2 ♣. Because you have two very promising major suits, it is right to open 2 ♣ on this hand despite the presence of "only" 21 points. Partner might easily pass a bid of 1 ♠ with a hand that would produce game in one suit or the other.

The Response to 2 ♣

The negative response to 2 ♣ is 2 ◇. This again is an artificial bid, bearing no relation to the responder's holding in diamonds. The responder bids 2 ◇ on all hands containing 0-6 points in high cards. Any other response to 2 ♣ is regarded as positive.

When the game-forcing 2 ♣ opening bid was first developed, the requirements for a positive response were somewhat stricter than they are now; in fact, they were so demanding that a negative response became almost inevitable. The modern tendency is to allow responder the freedom to give a positive response, either in a suit or in notrump, whenever he has 7 points or more. This treatment is to be recommended, for it is best if positive responses can be given more frequently.

For a positive response *in a suit*, however, it is still necessary that these points should include a certain quota of quick tricks. A positive response at the 2-level—2 ♡ or 2 ♠—should be based on at least one quick trick; for a response of 3 ♣ or 3 ◇, consuming an extra round of bidding, 1½ quick tricks are needed. Moreover, you should be quite chary about the way you *count* your quick tricks. An ace is one quick trick and a king is half a quick trick. But a K-Q combination may be counted as a whole trick only if it is in the suit that you are bidding; otherwise it should be counted as half a trick. To illustrate:

(1) ♠ K Q 8 4 3   ♡ 7 2   ◇ Q 7 4   ♣ 10 6 3
(2) ♠ J 4 2   ♡ K Q 9   ◇ K 8 7 4 2   ♣ 6 4

Hand (1) is worth a bid of 2 ♠ in response to 2 ♣: The hand contains the necessary seven points, and the K-Q combination may be counted as a quick trick since this is the suit you are bidding.

Hand (2), however, does not qualify for a bid of 3 ◇ over 2 ♣. For this positive response at the 3-level you need 1½ quick tricks, and the hand contains only one. The recommended response is therefore 2 NT, which is still a "positive" bid. In the same way, an A-Q combination may be counted as 1½ quick tricks only if it graces the suit that responder intends to bid.

When the requirements about quick tricks are faithfully adhered to, the 2 ♣ bidder is often able to see straightaway whether the responder's values will be useful to him. For example:

♠ A Q J 4 2   ♡ A K   ◇ A K 6   ♣ A J 4

If by happy chance your 2 ♣ opening is greeted with a response of 3 ♣, you can immediately place your partner with ♣ K-Q and ♠ K, which means that a contract of 7 NT must be very sound. The bidding would not be so easy if your methods were so loosely arranged that the 3 ♣ bid could be based on a motley assortment of queens and jacks.

It is inadvisable to bid a weak or moderate suit over 2 ♣. A holding such as K-10-9-x would be about the minimum for a response of 2 ♡ or 2 ♠, while for a 3-level response a reasonable five-card suit is required, such as Q-J-9-x-x.

When the responder has 7 or more points but lacks a biddable suit or has a poor quick-trick holding, he may bid notrump. A response of 2 NT suggests scattered values and 7-9 points; 3 NT shows 10-12.

Quiz on Responding to 2 ♣

Your partner opens 2 ♣. What is your response on each of the following hands?

(1) ♠ 7 5   ♡ A Q 9 7   ◇ 10 8 3   ♣ J 6 4 2
(2) ♠ J 8 6 4   ♡ A 2   ◇ K 10 7 5   ♣ J 5 3
(3) ♠ Q 10 7 5 3 2   ♡ K 4   ◇ 7 5   ♣ 10 9 8
(4) ♠ A 7 3   ♡ 8 3   ◇ Q 9 2   ♣ Q 9 8 7 3
(5) ♠ Q 10 7   ♡ 9 7 5   ◇ A Q 9 8 5   ♣ 7 4

Solutions

1. 2 ♡. You have only the minimum values for a positive response, but this bid at the 2-level does not waste any space and the useful heart suit is certainly worth mentioning.

2. 2 NT. This hand contains enough points and quick tricks for a positive response to 2 ♣, but the suits are not good enough for a bid of either 2 ♠ or 3 ◇. A response of 2 NT, showing scattered values and 7-9 points, affords a more accurate description of the hand.

3. 2 ◇. This hand is potentially quite strong opposite an opening 2 ♣, and it will assume considerable stature if partner can support spades or if the 2 ♣ opening is of the very strong balanced type. The first move, however, must be to warn partner about the scarcity of high cards by making the negative response of 2 ◇.

4. 2 NT. Once again the hand contains useful features, but it lacks 1½ quick tricks and the five-card suit is not strong enough for a bid at the 3-level. The most descriptive response is therefore 2 NT.

5. 3 ◇. This hand represents about the minimum strength on which it is advisable to hoist the bidding so high. To respond with 2 ◇, however, would represent false economy; no matter how strongly you bid later, you would never

succeed in convincing your partner that you held positive values and a biddable five-card suit.

Opener's Rebid After 2 ♣

When opener bids a suit after having opened with 2 ♣, he suggests an unbalanced hand and creates a forcing situation. The responder is entitled to presume that this suit consists of at least a powerful five-card suit. Moreover, if the opener makes a *jump* bid in a suit, he shows a *solid* suit—at least A-K-Q-J-x-x or A-K-Q-10-x-x-x, playable in a slam even opposite a void.

(1)	OPENER	RESPONDER		(2)	OPENER	RESPONDER
	2 ♣	2 ◇			2 ♣	2 ♡
	3 ♡				4 ♣	

In each case this jump rebid has the special meaning of setting the trump suit, so that a subsequent bid in a new suit by either player is control-showing. In (1) the responder, having already shown 0-6 points by his negative response, should try hard now to make an encouraging move if he has any worthwhile feature. Suppose he has this hand:

♠ 3 2   ♡ 10 4 3   ◇ K Q 7   ♣ 10 8 6 4 3

These values may well produce a slam opposite a game-going hand with a solid heart suit; responder should therefore bid 4 ◇. As the responder's hand is limited to less than seven points, opener should allow for the possibility that this bid shows a second-round control rather than the ace.

Over a positive response to 2 ♣, as in (2), it is more or less obligatory for opener to make a jump rebid whenever he has a solid suit, as this is such a valuable foundation for a slam sequence. Over 2 ◇, however, the jump rebid is restricted to those hands where slam is still possible despite the negative response.

Quiz on Opener's Rebid After 2 ♣

You open 2 ♣ and your partner responds 2 ♢. What is your rebid on the following hands?

(1) ♠ A J 9   ♡ A K Q 9 7   ♢ K Q 4   ♣ A 10
(2) ♠ K 4   ♡ A Q   ♢ A K Q 9 8 3   ♣ A J 10
(3) ♠ A K J 7   ♡ A Q J   ♢ 8   ♣ A K Q 8 2
(4) ♠ Q 7   ♡ A K Q J 7 5 3   ♢ A K Q   ♣ A
(5) ♠ A K Q 7 4   ♡ A K J 10 6   ♢ A Q   ♣ 5

Solutions

1. 2 NT. The temptation to rebid 2 ♡ should be resisted, as the hand is not quite strong enough for this forcing maneuver. A bid of 2 NT, showing 23 or 24 points, should provide a reasonably safe final contract if partner happens to be very weak.
2. 3 NT. The 3 NT rebid normally shows a balanced hand with 25 or 26 points, but it is a sound move on this hand as you can visualize nine likely tricks on almost any lead. It is right to go straight to the final contract, because if you were to bid 3 ♢ you might reach 3 NT with the strong hand exposed.
3. 3 ♣. There would be little point in bidding 2 ♠ with the object of saving space, as you intend to go to game in any event.
4. 3 ♡. A slam is still possible if you can find partner with first- or second-round spade control. You therefore make a jump rebid to set the trump suit and pave the way for a possible exchange of cue bids.
5. 2 ♠. Since you intend to tell partner all about this powerful two-suiter, it is right to follow the normal principle of bid-

ding the higher-ranking suit first, planning to bid and rebid
hearts later in order to accurately portray your 5-5 pattern.

Responder's Rebid After 2 ♣

After a 2 ♣ opening and a positive response, the bidding by
both players is developed along standard lines. There is one point
that is worth mentioning: A subsequent bid in notrump by the responding hand tends to be a denial of support for opener's suit rather
than an affirmation of all-round values.

OPENER	RESPONDER
2 ♣	2 ♡
2 ♠	2 NT

Responder holds:

♠ 8 5   ♡ A K 9 7   ◇ 8 5 4 2   ♣ 10 7 4

A bid of 2 NT in this sequence simply means that responder
has nothing more to contribute.

The responder's rebid after having made a *negative* response
tends to be a very vital point in the auction, particularly when he
proposes to support opener's suit. This is because a mistake at this
stage may result in a slam being missed or an unsound slam contract
being reached. In general, responder has the task of distinguishing
between three types of supporting hand. Suppose the bidding goes:

OPENER	RESPONDER
2 ♣	2 ◇
2 ♠	?

The scheme of raises of opener's suit is illustrated by these hands:

(1) ♠ J 9 7 3   ♡ 6 4   ◇ K 10 6 5   ♣ Q 7 3
(2) ♠ J 9 7 3   ♡ 6 4   ◇ Q 10 6 5   ♣ 8 7 3
(3) ♠ J 9 3   ♡ 10 6 4 3   ◇ 10 6 5   ♣ 8 7 3

With (1) the responder jumps to 4 ♠, showing good trump support and maximum values in the light of his initial response of 2 ◇. There is also an inference that the responder does not hold an ace or a void; with a first-round control he would raise to 3 ♠ and cue-bid on the next round.

With (2) the responder raises to 3 ♠, showing median values. Here he has good trump support and a potentially useful doubleton.

With (3) the responder still intends to support spades, but he first indicates the bombed-out nature of his hand by bidding 2 NT—a "Second Negative," as it is called. When the responder supports spades on the next round, opener will not get any wrong ideas.

When the responder cannot support opener's suit he should still look for an opportunity to show any useful features, which opposite a 2 ♣ opening may spell the difference between game and slam.

♠ 7 2   ♡ K 6 3   ◇ Q 7 5 3   ♣ J 8 4 2

The bidding is:

OPENER	RESPONDER
2 ♣	2 ◇
2 ♠	?

Responder should jump to 3 NT. This descriptive jump is safe, as responder has limited his hand to 0-6 points by bidding 2 ◇. If opener is gazing at a really powerful hand, he will greatly welcome this sign of life.

Similarly, the responder may feel free to introduce any potentially useful suit on the second round once he has responded negatively on the first. Thus:

♠ 7 2   ♡ Q J 6 5 3   ◇ Q 8 4   ♣ 7 6 2

After 2 ♣-2 ◇-2 ♠, the responder should bid 3 ♡; if he supinely bids 2 NT, his values may waste their sweetness on the desert air. The main advantage of restricting the negative 2 ◇ response to hands containing 0-6 points is that the responder can bid freely on the second round without overstating his values.

If the responder jumps in a new suit on the second round, he shows a suit that is solid apart from one card.

♠ 7 3   ♡ 9 5 4   ◇ K Q J 10 9 3   ♣ 10 7

After 2 ♣-2 ◇-2 ♠, this hand is portrayed by jumping to 4 ◇. If you should ever be so fortunate as to have a completely solid suit opposite an opening bid of 2 ♣, this can be shown by making a jump response on the *first* round.

WHEN OPENER HAS REBID AT NOTRUMP

It has been noted that after 2 ♣-2 ◇-2 NT, the responder may pass with a worthless hand; with 3 points, or with a suit as good as Q-x-x-x-x, he should push on to game.

In general, after a 2 ♣ opening and a rebid of 2 NT, the bidding may be developed along the same lines as after an opening bid of 2 NT. It is not proposed to cover these sequences here, as the purpose is to illustrate the mechanism of the 2 ♣ bid. The powerhouse sequences that occur when one player has shown a strong balanced hand are covered in Chapter 6.

STAYING OUT OF GAME AFTER 2 ♣

Although it was not always the standard practice, most players now arrange that the bidding may stop short of game if opener can do no more than rebid his suit after a Second Negative from partner.

(1)	OPENER	RESPONDER	(2)	OPENER	RESPONDER
	2 ♣	2 ♦		2 ♣	2 ♦
	2 ♥	2 NT		2 ♠	2 NT
	3 ♥			3 ♠	

In each case responder may pass. The advantage is that it is now possible to open 2 ♣ on a one-suited hand of this type:

♠ A K Q 10 8 4 3   ♥ 7   ♦ A K 5   ♣ 10 2.

After 2 ♣-2 ♦-2 ♠-2 NT, this hand can still be played in 3 ♠.

Add the queen of diamonds to opener's hand and he should jump to 4 ♠.

GETTING TO SLAM AFTER 2 ♣

When you are wondering whether you ought to bid slam, the vital question is not how strong your hand is but whether you have any reserves of strength beyond those you have already disclosed. A slam initiative after 2 ♣ does not necessarily have to come from the player with the big hand. Indeed, the skill with which the weaker hand is bid will generally be the deciding factor. Some illustrative sequences follow.

(1)

OPENER	RESPONDER
♠ A K Q 7 2	♠ 8 4
♡ A K 10 9 4	♡ J 8 7 5 3
◇ A Q 5	◇ 10 6 2
♣ —	♣ Q 8 4

OPENER	RESPONDER
2 ♣	2 ◇
2 ♠	2 NT (a)
3 ♡ (b)	5 ♡ (c)
6 ♡ (d)	Pass

The first three of these bids are routine. Then:

(a) Some players might bid 3 ♡ at this point. However, it is a useful principle that a suit introduced by the responding hand ought to be sturdy enough to provide a stopper at 3 NT opposite extreme shortage in the opener's hand.

(b) Opener has now shown his hand and intends to pass a raise to 4 ♡.

(c) If responder held an ace or a king, he might cue-bid it now and support hearts on the next round. As it is, the jump to 5 ♡ is the only way of showing that responder holds trump support and a key ruffing value in spades.

(d) As long as there is no trump loser, there must be a play for twelve tricks.

(2) OPENER   RESPONDER
    ♠ 10 5   ♠ K J 8 4 3
    ♡ A K   ♡ Q 10 6
    ◇ K Q J   ◇ A 8 4
    ♣ A K Q J 10 4   ♣ 8 2

    OPENER   RESPONDER
    2 ♣   2 ♠
    4 ♣ (a)   4 ◇ (b)
    4 ♡ (c)   4 NT (d)
    5 ♡   6 NT
    Pass

(a) Solid suit, at least six cards.
(b) and (c) Cue bids.
(d) Blackwood. It is unusual for the weaker hand to bid 4 NT
after a 2 ♣ opening, but here the responder has matters well in
hand. If opener has three aces and three kings, responder can count
the tricks for 7 NT; if a king is missing, he will still take a chance on
7 ♣, as opener may have ♠ Q or may be able to establish the
spades by ruffing. As it is, with an ace missing, responder bids
6 NT rather than 6 ♣, to protect the ♠ K.

Quiz on Responder's Rebid After 2 ♣

Partner opens 2 ♣ and rebids 2 ♡ over your response of 2 ◇.
What do you bid with each of the following hands?

(1) ♠ 7 5 4   ♡ 9 8 6 3   ◇ 8 7 6   ♣ 9 6 3
(2) ♠ 10 9 3   ♡ Q 10 7 5   ◇ 8 5   ♣ K 8 7 3
(3) ♠ Q 9 3   ♡ 6 4   ◇ K 7 5 2   ♣ J 10 8 5
(4) ♠ 6 5   ♡ Q 8 6 3   ◇ J 7 6   ♣ 10 7 5 4
(5) ♠ 10 3   ♡ 7 2   ◇ K 10 8 6 3   ♣ Q 9 5 2

Solutions

1. 2 NT. This is the Second Negative. You intend of course to support hearts, but first you must make discouraging noises. If you were to raise straightaway to 3 ♡, your partner might easily develop the fixation that you held better than a Yarborough.

2. 4 ♡. This direct raise to game shows maximum values, bearing in mind that your original response of 2 ◇ limits you to 6 points. It also denies an ace or a void.

3. 3 NT. This bid shows a few scattered points and may be all the encouragement your partner needs if he has been dealt a genuine rockcrusher. An unimaginative rebid of 2 NT could result in slam being missed.

4. 3 ♡. Because you have good trump support and a possible ruffing value you should give an immediate single raise rather than a Second Negative followed by a raise.

5. 3 ◇. Partner will place you with no more than 6 points for your initial response of 2 ◇, so you may safely show the good suit and fair values on the second round.

Ace Responses to 2 ♣ ("CAB")

Reversing the natural order of things, some players have developed methods of showing key cards in response to 2 ♣, leaving more mundane matters, such as the settlement of the trump suit, to be decided at a later date. One such method, from a system of bidding called "CAB" (Two Clubs, Aces, Blackwood), requires the responder to show his aces. The responses to 2 ♣ are as follows:

2 ◇	No aces; 0-7 points
2 ♡	Ace of hearts
2 ♠	Ace of spades
2 NT	No ace; 8+ points
3 ♣	Ace of clubs
3 ◇	Ace of diamonds
3 NT	Two aces
4 NT	Three aces

This scheme works well on powerful distributional hands where opener is interested primarily in his partner's controls. To exploit matters to the full, CAB players tend to open 2 ♣ on hands that would not qualify for this bid in standard methods.

♠ K Q 7 6 5   ♡ 7   ◇ A K Q J 9 8 3   ♣ —

This hand contains too few honor tricks for a standard opening of 2 ♣. Playing ace responses, however, opener may open 2 ♣ to discover at a safe level whether partner has ♠A.

As the responder's aces are shown immediately, a subsequent bid of 4 NT becomes a conventional request for kings—and this can be followed by 5 NT for queens. Once again, there undoubtedly are hands on which this is of considerable assistance to the opener.

So much for the advantages. The drawback is that there are many hands on which there are more important matters to be attended to than the discovery of the responder's aces. For example, if the strong hand contains no self-supporting suit, the first order of business should be to locate the best playable fit. In this case, the ace-showing response to 2 ♣ may cramp the auction: Responder may be forced to respond 3 ♣ if he has, for example, seven spades to the king and the singleton ♣ A! Moreover, the ace-showing response tells little about the overall strength of the responder's hand.

While it is always enlightening to know how many aces partner has, curiosity concerning these useful cards can perhaps be contained until more fundamental matters have been attended to. The standard scheme of responses to 2 ♣ more often conveys vital information at a more economical level.

4 NT After 2 ♣

The reader will agree, I've no doubt, that the ever-popular Blackwood Convention is seldom of much use to a player with a very big hand when he is interrogating the weak hand after a powerhouse 2 ♣ opening. After all, the responder to 2 ♣ tends to consider himself fortunate if he has one or more high honors of any kind. To devote the whole range of bids from 4 NT to 5 NT simply to ask him how many aces he holds is clearly a method that can be improved upon.

Regular partnerships, therefore, may consider a system of responses to 4 NT that will enable the weak hand to convey a great deal more information. One scheme of responses that has been tested and found satisfactory is this. If the 2 ♣ opener subsequently bids a conventional 4 NT, his partner replies as follows:

After a 2 ◇ response	*After a positive response to 2 ♣*
5 ♣ No king	One king
5 ◇ One king	Two kings
5 ♡ Two kings	One ace + values
5 ♠ One ace	One ace + one king *or*
	Three kings
5 NT One ace + values	Two aces *or*
	Four kings *or*
	One ace + two kings

The usefulness of this scheme can be seen in this example:

OPENER	RESPONDER
2 ♣	2 ◇
3 ♣	4 ♣
?	

Opener holds:

♠ A 4   ♡ A   ◇ A Q J 9   ♣ A K Q 9 6 2

Playing Blackwood and most other conventions, opener would be stymied—a bid of 4 NT would get him nowhere as this would ask for aces. Playing this convention, opener can bid 4 NT, for he is prepared to bid 6 ♣ if partner has one king. If this king is in spades or diamonds, twelve tricks will be highly probable. If it is in hearts, opener hopes he may be able to discard a spade on it and lose only one diamond trick.

The Forcing 2-Bid

The reader may have gathered that, like most tournament players, this writer considers the 2 ♣ opening bid to be far more efficient than the old-established method under which all opening 2-bids are forcing to game. However, the Forcing 2-bid is still popular with many rubber-bridge players, and there are those who would gladly burn every copy of this book if it were ignored.

The requirements for a 2-bid are the same as for a 2 ♣ opening, with one important exception. It is not possible to arrange for the bidding to be halted in 2 NT, as this is the conventional negative response. Balanced hands of 23 or 24 points, therefore, are not opened with a 2-bid but with the non-forcing bid of 2 NT. The minimum balanced hand for a Forcing 2-bid is 25 points.

According to the most popular scheme, a positive response to a 2-bid may be given with at least 7 points, including distribution, provided the hand contains one quick trick. If only half a quick trick is present, 8 points are needed. When these requirements are not met, the negative response of 2 NT must be given. Thereafter the bidding continues to game, except when the opener rebids the same suit after a negative response.

OPENER	RESPONDER
2 ♠	2 NT
3 ♠	?

Now the responder may pass with a worthless hand.

An immediate single raise of opener's suit is a positive bid and may be the first move in a slam investigation. An immediate double raise has a special meaning, showing good trump support but no ace or king and no singleton. After a 2-bid in a major suit, especially, less space is available than after a 2 ♣ opening, and it is not possible to provide for a Second Negative response.

Devotees of the Forcing 2-bid can point to two advantages over the artificial 2 ♣ bid. First, the Forcing 2-bid will tend to come out better if the lefthand opponent is able to make some enormous preemptive jump over the opening bid; while the 2 ♣ opening will have done no more than announce a powerhouse hand, the Forcing

2-bid will also have mentioned a possible trump suit. The second and more important point is that the Forcing 2-bid makes the bidding easier on strong hands oriented around a minor suit.

♠ 8   ♡ A K 5   ◇ A K J 10 7   ♣ A K Q 8

Playing the Forcing 2-bid, the bidding will start with 2 ◇ -2 NT-3 ♣. The partnership is now well placed to select the best contract. If the hand is opened with an artificial 2 ♣, however, opener may find himself in poor shape on the third round: after 2 ♣-2 ◇ -3 ◇ -3 ♠, for example, opener will no longer be able to show the club suit without venturing beyond the safe haven of 3 NT.

The case *against* the Forcing 2-bid, however, is almost overwhelming. It is uneconomical, as it it uses four opening bids instead of one to introduce a game-forcing hand; the 2 ♣ opening releases the other opening 2-bids for other purposes. No player who has become addicted either to Weak Twos in the majors or to strong Intermediate Twos would willingly give them up in order to return to Forcing 2-bids.

In addition, the negative response of 2 NT is inefficient in two ways. First, it is wasteful of space. More serious, it often leads to a notrump contract being played from the wrong side, with the strong hand displayed on the table. This is invariably greatly appreciated by the defenders and also results in the opening lead coming through, rather than into, any tenaces held by the opening bidder. This disadvantage of the Forcing Two can be minimized if the partnership employs the Herbert Convention. The negative response to the opening 2-bid is then a bid of *the cheapest available suit*. Thus over 2 ♣ the negative response is 2 ◇ , over 2 ◇ the negative is 2 ♡; over 2 ♠ the negative is not 2 NT but 3 ♣. With the values for a positive response, the responder bids normally unless his suit is the "Herbert" suit, in which case he bids 2 NT. The adoption of this method is recommended to players who favor the Forcing 2-bid.

Still another disadvantage of the Forcing 2-bid is that it shows up poorly on powerhouse hands where the main strength is in a major suit; unexpectedly, the artificial 2 ♣ opening actually saves a round of bidding in such a case.

♠ A K J 8 5   ♡ A K Q 9   ◊ 7   ♣ A Q 5

Playing Forcing 2-bids, the auction begins with
2 ♠-2 NT-3 ♡. Now the responding hand cannot bid clubs, which
may represent the best trump suit, without venturing beyond 3 NT.
If the opening bid is an artificial 2 ♣, however, the sequence will
be 2 ♣-2 ◊-2 ♠. The responder then has an additional round of
bidding in which to disclose his treasures.

Finally, as we have seen, the 2 ♣ opening works better on
strong, balanced hands. Many players have given up Forcing 2-bids
in favor of the artificial 2 ♣, but I have known no one to give up the
2 ♣ bid in favor of Forcing 2-bids.

Intermediate (Acol) 2-Bids

When the artificial 2 ♣ opening is in use, opening bids of
2 ◊, 2 ♡ and 2 ♠ are available for other purposes. Many players
use these bids as weak openings, based on a six-card suit headed by
at least Q-J-10 and a total of about 6-11 high-card points, including
1½ quick tricks. The case for the Weak Two is powerful: In addition
to its preemptive effect, when used with discipline it can lead to
some accurate constructive sequences on those occasions when
partner, rather than the opponents, has most of the outstanding
strength. The Weak Two, however, does not come within the scope
of this book.

Another method, also popular, is to use the bids of 2 ◊, 2 ♡
and 2 ♠ to cover strong distributional hands that are not quite rich
enough in high cards to open with 2 ♣ but that may nevertheless
produce a game opposite a partner *who would pass a bid of one in a
suit.* This method derives from the British Acol system, but it fits
equally well with Standard American.

Intermediate 2-bids do not themselves occur frequently, but
they affect the bidding of many other hands. When partner opens
with a bid of one you need not strain to keep the bidding open on the

smell of an oil rag, as partner would have opened an Intermediate Two if he held nearly a game in his own hand.

REQUIREMENTS FOR AN INTERMEDIATE 2-BID

The bids 2 ◇, 2 ♡ and 2 ♠ are forcing for one round, based usually on at least a strong six-card suit and eight or more likely tricks, or on a powerful two-suited hand, 5-4 at the very least. An Intermediate Two is likely to contain between 16-19 high-card points, but this criterion is applied flexibly. When you are not sure whether to open with one or two, the tests to apply are these:

(a) If you open with a one-bid and this is passed out, will there be a danger that you have missed game?

(b) Is your hand so strong that if you open with a one-bid and partner responds, you will have difficulty in portraying the full strength of your hand on the next round?

If there is an affirmative answer to either of these questions, it is likely that your hand is suitable for an Intermediate 2-bid. Let us look at some examples.

(1) ♠ A Q J 10 8   ♡ A K J 7 2   ◇ K J   ♣ 7
(2) ♠ K Q J 9 8 3   ♡ 7 2   ◇ —   ♣ A K J 10 5
(3) ♠ A Q J 9 5 4   ♡ 8   ◇ A K 7 2   ♣ A 4
(4) ♠ A K Q J 10 4   ♡ A 7 2   ◇ 8   ♣ K Q 5

Each hand should be opened with 2 ♠, for in each case it is not difficult to imagine responding hands with which partner will pass a bid of 1 ♠ but which will produce a cold game. On (4), moreover, your problems would not be over even if your partner did respond to 1 ♠, for no rebid could even begin to do justice to such a powerful hand. Since none of these hands qualify for a game-forcing opening of 2 ♣, a bid of 2 ♠, forcing for one round only, is the ideal solution.

Quiz on Intermediate (Acol) 2-Bids

Playing Intermediate 2-bids, what do you open with the following hands?

(1) ♠ A 6 2   ♡ 7   ◇ A K Q 6 5 4 3   ♣ 10 6

(2) ♠ 8   ♡ A K 9 3   ◇ A K 7 5 4   ♣ A Q 2

(3) ♠ A J 3   ♡ A K Q 10 9 5   ◇ 7   ♣ A K 4

(4) ♠ A Q J 4   ♡ —   ◇ A K 10 9 7 5   ♣ A K 2

(5) ♠ A 7   ♡ 10 7 3   ◇ A K Q 10 7 6 4 2   ♣ —

Solutions

1. 1 ◇. This hand contains eight likely tricks but is not strong enough in high cards for 2 ◇. (As game in a minor suit is hard to make, an Intermediate Two in diamonds tends to contain at least *nine* tricks rather than eight.) The hand can be represented by opening 1 ◇ and jumping to 3 ◇ on the next round, although it is only fair to admit that you might bid the same way with one diamond fewer.

2. 1 ◇. This is an awkward hand to deal with in any system, and it must be conceded that Intermediate 2-bids do not make it any easier. The hand is simply not strong enough for an Intermediate 2 ◇ followed by a forcing bid of 3 ♡ on the next round.

3. 2 ♣. This hand is too strong for an opening bid of 2 ♡. Little help is needed for a slam contract, and your partner is more likely to enter into the spirit of things by bidding such a holding as ♣ Q-J-x-x-x if you open 2 ♣ than if you open 2 ♡ and rebid 4 ♡ over 2 NT.

4. 2 ◇. An Intermediate 2-bid is forcing for only one round, but there is no rooted objection to employing it also on hands where game is certain to be reached. Here the bidding will proceed more smoothly if you start with 2 ◇ rather than 2 ♣, as you are showing your main suit at once.

5. 2 ◇. In terms of high cards this hand is below par. But it has so many tricks that you could not possibly rebid it accurately if you opened with 1 ◇.

RESPONDING TO AN INTERMEDIATE 2-BID

The traditional negative response to an Intermediate 2-bid is 2 NT. But, as was seen when discussing Forcing 2-bids, "Herbert" negatives are actually more efficient and are therefore recommended.

For a positive response in a new suit you need slightly higher values than when responding to 2 ♣: 10 or more points, unless you have good trump support or can show a biddable suit at the 2-level.

A response in a new suit shows a strong four-card suit at the 2-level or a good five-card suit at the 3-level. Because opener's suit is likely to be so powerful, you do not bid poor suits in response to an Intermediate Two. Suppose your partner opens 2 ♡ and you have these hands:

(1) ♠ K Q 9 2   ♡ 8 3   ◇ K 10   ♣ J 8 5 4 3
(2) ♠ K 8 4   ♡ 7 4   ◇ Q 10 8 7 3   ♣ A J 2

With (1) it is better to respond with 2 ♠ than with 3 ♣. The hand is unlikely to be played in either of your suits, so the important thing is to show where your high cards are. With (2), a jump to 3 NT, suggesting a scattered 10 or 11 points, is better than 3 ◇.

As an Intermediate 2-bid opening is invariably based on a good suit, the responder may feel free to raise on as little as x-x-x, Q-x or even J-x. An important requirement is that a raise to three of the opener's suit is a positive response and guarantees an ace; this is a useful aid in slam sequences. With the values for a positive raise but no ace, you jump to four in opener's suit. When you have trump support and little else, so that you can see that a slam is out of the question, you avoid overheating your partner by first giving the negative response.

♠ J 7 4   ♡ Q 10 8 3   ◇ K 8 2   ♣ 10 9 7

Over partner's 2 ♡ you are very willing to undertake a game, but first you respond with the "Herbert" negative of 2 ♠.

Quiz on Responses to Intermediate 2-Bids

Your partner opens with an Intermediate 2 ♠. What do you respond with each of the following hands? (You are playing "Herbert" negatives.)

(1) ♠ J 7 3   ♡ Q 10 3   ◇ A Q J 5 3   ♣ 8 4
(2) ♠ 8 7 5   ♡ K J 8 5 4   ◇ 9 8 3 2   ♣ 10
(3) ♠ Q 4   ♡ K J 4   ◇ A 10 5   ♣ J 9 6 5 3
(4) ♠ Q 8 3 2   ♡ K 7 2   ◇ 8 2   ♣ K J 7 5
(5) ♠ 10 7 4   ♡ K 8 3   ◇ K J 3   ♣ Q J 8 5

Solutions

1. 3 ◇. This hand represents about the minimum for a positive response at the 3-level, justified because you are able to show a very sound suit.
2. 3 ♣. You intend to reach game with this useful supporting hand, but it is advisable to begin with a negative response. An immediate raise to 3 ♠ would guarantee an ace, and the hand is not strong enough in high cards for a bid of 3 ♡.
3. 3 ♠. A doubleton honor represents sound support for an Intermediate 2-bid, and this single raise has the additional merit of indicating an ace somewhere in the hand. To re-

spond 3 ♣ with this ragged club suit is not in accordance with the convention.

4. 4 ♠. The double raise shows a sprinkling of high cards and good trump support, but denies an ace. If, after this raise, your partner nevertheless expresses interest in a slam, you may cue-bid your kings without fear of misunderstanding.

5. 3 NT. As you have all-round strength and no ruffing values, this gives a better description than a raise to 4 ♠. The jump to 3 NT does not necessarily imply a shortage in partner's suit.

DEVELOPING THE BIDDING AFTER AN INTERMEDIATE 2-BID

A positive response to an Intermediate Two establishes a game-forcing situation and the bidding proceeds on standard lines. A jump rebid by the opener shows a solid suit and does not necessarily indicate extra values. Suppose you open 2 ♡ with this hand and partner bids 3 ♣:

♠ A K 10   ♡ A K Q J 9 2   ◊ 8 3   ♣ Q 5

You have no more than the required eight tricks for your Intermediate Two, but the queen of clubs is sure to be a valuable card. Therefore you should not fail to jump to 4 ♡, setting the suit and leaving your partner in control. The jump rebid with this type hand is always a helpful move. When the opener does not jump in this way, his partner may infer that the suit is not solid.

After a simple raise on the first round, implying an ace, the opener may cue-bid if he is interested in a slam and wants his partner to identify this ace. After an immediate jump raise, denying an ace, a cue bid by the opener will necessarily guarantee at least three first-round controls: the responder may now freely begin to cue-bid kings.

OPENER	RESPONDER
♠ A K 10 7 5 3	♠ Q 8 6 2
♡ A Q J 2	♡ K 4
◊ A 10	◊ K 8 3
♣ 7	♣ Q 9 3 2

OPENER	RESPONDER
2 ♠	4 ♠
5 ◊	5 ♡ (a)
6 ♠ (b)	Pass

(a) Responder is encouraged by his partner's 5 ◊ bid, as he now knows that ◊ K is "working." His bid of 5 ♡ shows the king, as he has already denied any ace.

(b) Placing his partner with ♡ K, opener can be fairly hopeful that the only loser will be a club. If partner does not have ◊ K, his diamond losers may go away on the hearts.

After a *negative* response to an Intermediate Two, a jump rebid by opener does not show a solid suit. Opener is merely saying that his hand is strong enough for game in its own right.

OPENER	RESPONDER
2 ♡	2 ♠ ("Herbert" negative)
4 ♡	

Responder is expected to pass this jump rebid, even if he has some useful values. And it goes without saying that you never disturb partner on weakness. Suppose, in the sequence above, that this is your hand:

♠ Q 10 9 7 4 3 2   ♡ —   ◊ 10 8 5   ♣ 7 6 2

Although you have not yet bid spades in a natural sense, you must pass. Partner has said that he can make 4 ♡, and it will be best to leave him with his illusions.

After a negative response to an Intermediate Two, a simple

rebid by the opener is not forcing, but the responder will normally raise to game if he has as much as one trick—an ace, or a K-Q or a ruffing value.

A simple change of suit by the opener, however, is forcing.

OPENER	RESPONDER
2 ♥	2♠ ("Herbert" negative)
3 ♦	

Responder may not pass in this sequence. If he raises opener's second suit this tends to be encouraging. But a simple return to the first suit may denote a blizzard, and the responder should avoid this bid if his hand possesses any useful features. A degree of imagination is called for, based on the fact that the opener is likely to have ten or even eleven cards in his two suits. In the sequence above, suppose that you are the responder with these cards:

(1) ♠ 10 8 7 3 2   ♥ 10 4   ♦ Q 10 2   ♣ 9 8 6
(2) ♠ Q 7 6 4 2   ♥ 9   ♦ 8 4   ♣ Q 8 6 3 2

With (1), you should jump to 4 ♥ over 3 ♦! The trump support is tolerable, and the diamond holding is certain to be worth a trick. With (2), by contrast, you hate every moment, as your two black queens are probably quite useless. You therefore bid 3 ♥, the weakest possible call. If you ever seriously contemplated bidding 3 NT with this second hand, you would be well advised not to play Intermediate Twos.

Other Strong Openings

Bridge theorists like to put every possible bid to work, and a use has therefore been found for the exotic openings of 4 NT and five of a major suit.

In days of yore an opening bid of 4 NT showed a balanced rockcrusher, about 28-30 points. Such a hand can now be shown by

opening with 2 ♣ and jumping to 4 NT over a negative response of
2 ◊. The most productive use of a 4 NT opening, therefore, is as
an ace-asking bid. The responses are as follows:

5 ♣	No ace
5 ◊	Ace of diamonds
5 ♡	Ace of hearts
5 ♠	Ace of spades
5 NT	Two aces
6 ♣	Ace of clubs

Unless you happen to be fortune's child, you really cannot
expect to have very many opportunities to use this convention.
Ideally, opener needs something like this:

♠ —   ♡ K Q J 10 8 6 3 2   ◊ A K Q 10   ♣ A

With this hand, normal Blackwood does not help, and an attempt to develop the hand slowly may invite heavy interference. A
direct bid of 4 NT will disclose whether partner has the vital ♡ A.

THE 5 ♡ AND 5 ♠ OPENINGS

The opening bid of five of a major suit has been described as
the rarest bid in bridge. It shows a hand in which the only losers are
the ace and king of the trump suit. The responder is invited to raise
once for each key card he holds.

♠ Q J 10 9 7 5 4 2   ♡ A K   ◊ —   ♣ A K Q

If you ever hold this hand, you should open 5 ♠. Partner,
when he recovers his poise, will disregard any useless honors he has
in the other suits. He will raise to 6 ♠ if he has either the ace or
king of spades; or to 7 ♠ if he has both the ace and king.

3

Powerhouse Responses and Rebids

♠ ♡ ◇ ♣

The Jump-Shift Response to 1 ♣, 1 ◇, 1 ♡ or 1 ♠—Developing the Bidding After a Jump Shift—Other Strong Responses to a One-bid —Powerhouse Rebids by Opener

Strength in a vacuum can be virtually useless. Opener may hold half the points in the deck, but if partner is busted and has no card of entry, the result can be very disappointing. It is only strength in intimate combination with strength in the hand opposite that is more or less guaranteed to produce significant results.

Thus some of the very strongest powerhouse sequences occur when one player has quite an ordinary opening hand and his partner has a good hand opposite. Or when opener has a promising hand that assumes immense proportions when a bid of one is met with a favorable response. In each case a jump shift may be the best move, as in these sequences:

(1)	OPENER	RESPONDER		(2)	OPENER	RESPONDER
	1 ◇	2 ♠			1 ♡	1 ♠
					3 ♣	

In each sequence the message is, "The curfew shall not ring tonight." A jump shift is unconditionally forcing to game and has no upper limit. No hand is too powerful to be expressed by a jump

45

shift—though some responding hands, as we shall see, are so strong that a different method of development may work more fluently.

The reader should at this point be warned that a small numbei of players use the jump-shift response as a very weak, preemptive bid based on a six-card or longer suit. The author has heard this practice well spoken of by some rubber-bridge players on their way to the bankruptcy court, but its use is in no sense standard. It was in fact devised for use in duplicate competitions, where the struggle for part-score hands is more intense than at team play or rubber bridge. Even there it is not clear that weak jump responses confer an overall gain in efficiency.

The Jump-shift Response to
1 ♣, 1 ◇, 1 ♡ or 1 ♠

There has always been some difference of opinion concerning the freedom with which this response should be used. Many good judges consider that it should be reserved for hands of 19 points or more, where there is a definite whiff of slam in the air. "There is no need," they maintain, "to jump the bidding with every hand where game-going values are present; a forcing situation can, if necessary, be created on the second round by a change of suit or by a jump bid. By restricting the use of the jump-shift response to really powerful hands, you alert partner at once to the likelihood of a slam."

A second school of thought maintains that since a jump shift is forcing only to game and not to slam, it should be employed whenever game-going values are known to be present. Thus the responder should almost invariably employ a jump shift when he has 16 points or more, including distribution, and especially when he has a good fit in opener's suit. "It is false economy," these players contend, "to make a cheap response on the first round and then be obliged to jump on the second round in an attempt to catch up." They add with some justification that the failure to make an im-mediate jump shift may also leave responder stranded on the second round, with no satisfactory way of expressing his values. Suppose the opening bid is 1 ◇ and the responder holds:

(1) ♠ A 10 9   ♡ K Q J 10 8 2   ◇ A 2   ♣ 9 8
(2) ♠ A K J 8   ♡ K 8 4   ◇ Q 3   ♣ A J 9 5

With the first hand nothing is gained by bidding only 1 ♡ over 1 ◇. If opener continues with 2 ◇, responder is obliged to force now with 3 ♡. Thus he has reached the same level, with the disadvantage that he has not disclosed such a strong hand as this.

With the second hand suppose the responder, over the opening bid of 1 ◇, begins with what may appear to be the economical bid of 1 ♠. Opener rebids 2 ◇, let us say, and responder has to keep things going by bidding 3 ♣. This is already a misleading way of showing such a balanced hand—and responder's problems are not yet over. If opener gives preference to 3 ♠, does responder bring matters to a close by bidding 3 NT? And if opener bids 3 NT over 3 ♣, does responder intend to pass, or does he make one last try by bidding a quantitative 4 NT? All these problems can be avoided by forcing with 2 ♠, after which any question of slam may be safely left to opener.

In this difference of approach, it is clear that each side can back itself with good arguments. We will therefore aim to enjoy the best of both worlds.

WHO'S TO BE CAPTAIN?

In general there are two strategies for bidding any bridge hand: try to describe your own hand, leaving partner to determine the best contract, or endeavor to gain a clear picture of partner's hand, so that you yourself can ultimately make the vital decision.

Most hands fall into familiar patterns, and players do not often have to exercise a conscious choice. But when, in response to your partner's opening, you are undecided whether to force or not, it is a very sound idea to ask yourself, before selecting the first response, which approach is better suited to your hand. If you think it will be better to paint partner a picture of your hand, it will generally be right to disclose your strength by means of a jump shift. If instead you plan to be the captain, it may be right to keep the bidding low. Your partner opens 1 ♠ and you hold:

♠ K 4   ♡ A Q J 10 9 3   ◇ Q J 10   ♣ Q 3

It does not seem that you ought to take charge with this hand. There is no problem about game, but it is hard to see how you yourself can discover, at a safe level, whether your partner has the first- or second-round controls in clubs and diamonds that would be needed for slam. Therefore it is right to force at once with 3 ♡, intending to bid 4 ♡ on the next round and leaving partner in charge. This sequence will show your limitations as well as your strength, for when a player makes a game bid in a forcing situation there is always an inference that he cannot himself initiate a slam venture.

WHEN YOU SHOULD FORCE FREELY

Accordingly, when you intend that your partner shall become the captain, you should be willing to force quite freely, with 16 points or even slightly less. Do this whenever you think you will be able to express the main features of your hand in one or two bids. The next example is similar in some ways to the previous hand. Your partner opens with 1 ♠ and you hold:

♠ A J 10 4   ♡ 10 9   ◇ 9 4   ♣ A K Q J 6

With such poor holdings in diamonds and hearts, how will you ever be able to tell that there are not two quick losers in these suits? (You may be lucky enough to find partner with two aces, of course, but a skillful bidder does not give up on slam solely because one ace is missing.) You should force at once, therefore, with 3 ♣. There is then no way you can become embarrassed, for over a rebid of 3 ◇ or 3 ♡ you intend to bid 4 ♠. The message will be: "I have a fine club suit and I have strong spade support, and that's about all. I have no great extra values, for then I would not have made a bid that permits you to pass. Nor have I any vital controls in the unbid suits, which I might have shown had I proceeded more slowly.''

Note the value of the negative inference. This general style of bidding may be termed "getting the hand off your chest," and it can be very effective indeed.

When you do not have strong support for opener's suit, you should still be willing to consider a force whenever you have as many as 16 points in high cards, even if you have only a four-card suit, provided that your hand will be suitable for a bid in notrump on the next round. Your partner opens 1 ♣ and you hold:

♠ Q J 4 2   ♡ A K 10 6   ◇ K Q 2   ♣ Q 4

Force at once with 2 ♡, disclosing your full strength. If your partner continues with 2 NT, 3 ♣ or 3 ♡, you can complete the picture of your hand very nicely indeed by bidding 3 NT. Partner is left in control, with a good idea of the combined assets.

It is usually right to force with any powerhouse hand that contains a six-card suit. Suppose your partner opens with 1 ♠ and you hold:

♠ 10 9   ♡ A K J 10 6 3   ◇ A 2   ♣ Q 10 4

Here you jump to 3 ♡. This hand represents, of course, a rock-bottom minimum for a jump shift, and you intend to continue with 4 ♡, saying, in effect, "Over and out."

WHEN NOT TO FORCE WITH A POWERHOUSE

You are naturally not obliged to voice a jump shift every time you have a big hand. A simple bid in a new suit by a player who has not previously passed is forcing, if only for one round, and sometimes this represents a more convenient approach. (Should your partner ever pass such a bid, you may look to a higher law to punish him. But you should not, out of anticipation of such a crime, distort your own bidding.)

So, no matter how strong your hand, you do not have to jump if your judgment tells you that this is not the best way of extracting vital information. It is certainly *normal* to make a jump shift when you have an enormous responding hand, but this principle is not applied with the same inflexibility as the laws of the Medes and the Persians. Suppose that you are fortunate enough to hold this delightful hand and your partner opens the bidding with 1 ♡ or one of a minor:

♠ A Q 10 8 5   ♡ A 4   ◇ K J 10   ♣ A Q 4

With such a hand you are on your way to a slam the moment partner opens; the only uncertain factors are how high and in which denomination. A simple response of 1 ♠ will almost certainly elicit more information about partner's hand than a jump shift of 2 ♠!

In effect, as you cannot hope to portray the strength of this hand in all its glory, so that partner can judge, you plan to take charge. The best initial strategy is to take things quietly and allow partner to tell you all he can about his hand. *You will find that opener's rebid tends to be more informative after a simple response than over a jump shift.* Observe these two sequences, one where responder has forced and one where he has not:

(1)	OPENER	RESPONDER		(2)	OPENER	RESPONDER
	1 ♡	1 ♠			1 ♡	2 ♠
	3 ♠				3 ♠	

In (1) opener's jump to 3 ♠ clearly defines his hand: He has 17-19 points, and he surely has four-card support for spades as it is a firm principle not to afford jump support with only three trumps. But what of the raise to 3 ♠ in the second sequence? Is this similarly based, or is opener merely making compulsory noises with a minimum hand and perhaps only three-card support for what he presumes to be a good suit? Responder clearly obtains more information by bidding only 1 ♠ initially, allowing his partner to make a free rather than a forced rebid. Similarly:

(1)	OPENER	RESPONDER		(2)	OPENER	RESPONDER
	1 ♡	2 ♣			1 ♡	3 ♣
	2 ♡				3 ♡	

In (1) it is clear that opener has a minimum or near-minimum hand. He cannot, for example, have the 17-19 points and strong six-card suit with which the standard move would be to jump to 3 ♡. In (2) no such inference can be drawn: Opener would not make a jump rebid over the force on such a holding as A-J-10-x-x-x, no matter how strong the rest of his hand might be, for it is a hard-and-fast rule that such a jump in a forcing situation shows a solid suit. Here too, then, opener's rebid is more definitive over the simple response than over the force.

The principle is clear. Do not waste space in starting to paint a picture if your hand is so strong that you cannot hope to complete this picture. Instead, make a simple response in a suit, leaving partner with freedom to tell you more about his hand.

There is another common situation where it may be better not to force: You have a powerful two-suited hand and an immediate jump shift would consume too much space.

♠ 7 5   ♡ A K Q 7   ◊ A Q J 8 4   ♣ Q 3

Suppose that your partner opens with 1 ♠ and you force with 3 ◊. The auction may continue like this:

OPENER	RESPONDER
1 ♠	3 ◊
3 ♠	?

Do you hide the hearts at this point and bid 3 NT, which might after all be the only makable game contract? Or do you see it through by bidding 4 ♡, hoping that partner will be able to handle this development? Either way, there is no guarantee that you will reach the right contract. The hand is easier to cope with if you start with a simple bid of 2 ◊ over 1 ♠, for now no rebid by opener will embarrass you: Over 2 ♠ from partner you can continue with a forcing bid of 3 ♡ on the next round. Similarly:

♠ J 3   ♡ K 4   ◊ A K 7 5 3   ♣ A Q J 10

Opposite an opening bid of 1 ♡ or 1 ♠, a jump to 3 ◊ will leave you in difficulty if opener rebids his major suit. To bid 4 ♣ now would take the partnership beyond range of 3 NT; yet a slam may be missed if this club suit is not shown. (There is one more theoretical drawback to this sequence: After the auction 1 ♡-3 ◊-3 ♡-4 ♣, opener may interpret 4 ♣ as a cue bid, agreeing on his heart suit. As we shall see later, some hands are hard to bid accurately unless such a cue bid may be made.) By beginning with 2 ◊, responder gains a clearer definition of opener's values and also ensures that it will be possible to show both minor suits at a safe level.

To sum up, do not feel that you are obliged to force with a powerhouse responding hand when (a) your hand is so enormously strong that it will be easier to get partner to limit his hand than for you to limit yours or (b) a force will make it impossible to show a two-suited hand below the level of 3 NT.

WHICH SUIT TO FORCE IN

When the responder makes a jump shift, it is natural to force in the same suit as you would have selected for a simple response.

♠ K 10 6 3   ♡ A Q 7 2   ◊ 7   ♣ A K Q 4

Over an opening bid of 1 ◇, the response is 2 ♡. It is clearly going to be important to locate any available 4-4 fit, and the responder should follow the normal principle of bidding his four-card suits "up the line."

There is, however, another bidding principle that sometimes conflicts: You should not bid poor or moderate suits in very strong hands. There is a very sound reason for this prohibition. When you have a major suit consisting of, say, A-x-x-x opposite J-x-x-x, you may be able to afford to lose two tricks in this suit and still have a very satisfactory play for game. Such a combination, however, does not afford a satisfactory foundation at all for a slam contract. Therefore in all strong hands where a slam may be on the horizon, avoid bidding a suit that you would have misgivings about playing in if raised. Thus:

♠ A K J 2   ♡ Q 7 5 4   ◇ A 6   ♣ K 10 6

Over partner's 1 ♣ or 1 ◇ opening, the response is not 2 ♡ but 2 ♠. You would be very willing to play in hearts with this hand if partner were to introduce the suit, but it would be poor tactics to bid 2 ♡ now; if you did, you would never feel able to play in this suit with full confidence that it did not include two losers.

In line with this, it can even be right to bid a non-existent suit in preference to a moderate suit. Partner opens 1 ♠ and you hold:

♠ K Q   ♡ A 10 8 3   ◇ K 10 6 2   ♣ A J 10

If you start with 3 ◇ or 3 ♡ and partner raises, you will not fancy playing in this suit. The only way to reach a contract of 6 ◇ or 6 ♡ in safety is by beginning with 3 ♣! Then if partner bids a red suit you can support it. Of course, you do not intend to play in clubs in any circumstances. If your partner raises you to 4 ♣, this will mean that he has at least a five-card spade suit, so you may continue with 4 ♠.

Quiz on Jump-Shift Responses

Your partner opens 1 ♡. What is your response with each of the following hands?

(1) ♠ A Q 7 5 2   ♡ 7 3   ◇ J 2   ♣ A K Q 10
(2) ♠ A K J 10 3   ♡ 7 2   ◇ K J 4   ♣ A 9 7
(3) ♠ Q 4 2   ♡ A Q 8   ◇ A K J 7 2   ♣ 7 5
(4) ♠ 8 3 2   ♡ J 2   ◇ A K J 10   ♣ A Q J 5
(5) ♠ Q J 9 7 5   ♡ A   ◇ A K   ♣ A Q 7 4 3

Solutions

1. 1 ♠. It is tempting to jump to 2 ♠ with a hand of this strength, but if you do you may not be able to bid clubs below the level of 3 NT. This excellent club suit is a feature you should be unwilling to suppress, so it is better to keep the bidding one level lower.

2. 2 ♠. This time the immediate jump shift is a very satisfactory move, as it expresses the full strength of your hand and, when followed by a rebid in notrump on the next round, will leave partner in a good position to select the final contract.

3. 3 ◇. Unless you force with this hand, with the intention of supporting hearts on the next round, it will be hard to convince partner that you have so many key cards. You have only to ask yourself what the next move would be if the auction started 1 ♡-2 ◇-2 ♡ to realize that an immediate jump shift will make life very much easier. Moreover, because you lack controls in the black suits, the right approach is to plan to bid the full strength of your hand and leave partner in charge.

4. 2 ◇. With this hand you plan to show both your suits and leave partner to select the contract. In order to stay within range of 3 NT, you must start with 2 ◇, so that you can bid

3 ♣ over a rebid of 2 ♡. If your partner's next bid over 3 ♣ is 3 ♡, you intend to raise to 4 ♡, which will surely be the right contract.

5. 1 ♠. This hand is so strong that you can hardly hope to convey its tremendous power and distribution. It is therefore better to plan a series of forcing bids that will allow partner to tell you all about his hand. In effect you are deciding, at the outset, that you are going to be the captain.

Developing the Bidding After a Jump Shift

When the opener's bid of one of a suit is met by a jump-shift response, opener often continues as he would have done over a simple response, although necessarily one level higher.

OPENER	RESPONDER
1 ♣	2 ◇
?	

Opener holds:

♠ 10 6 5   ♡ K Q 7 2   ◇ 4 2   ♣ A K J 4

There are some players who favor the unspeakable bid of 2 NT in this situation, imagining that this is necessary in order to warn partner of a minimum opening. This is wrong, however. A rebid in notrump over a force simply shows, in general, the type of hand with which opener would have bid 1 NT over a simple response.

Here, over a 1 ◇ response, the opener would have bid 1 ♡, so now he should bid 2 ♡, which for the moment gives no indication of his point count: Opener may be strong or he may, as here, have a minimum hand. One of the first objects of good bidding is to find a suitable trump fit, and this is still a general objective after a jump shift, although with the caveat previously noted: You do not introduce a weak four-card suit when there is an aroma of slam in the air.

OPENER   RESPONDER
1 ♣   2 ♡
?

Opener holds:

♠ J 9 7 4   ♡ K 7   ◊ A J 5   ♣ K Q 9 3

Over a response of 1 ♡ opener would have bid 1 ♠ , despite the weakness of his holding in this suit. As it is, the paramount consideration is to avoid a slam with two losers in the trump suit. The best bid therefore is 2 NT, showing a sound opening with all-round values.

REBID OF OPENER'S SUIT

A simple rebid of opener's suit over a force is unlimited: It may mask a strong hand or a complete minimum. This wide range is necessary, for the opener cannot show a strong one-suited hand by means of a jump rebid, as he might over a simple response.

♠ A 2   ♡ K J 10 8 6 3   ◊ A Q 9   ♣ Q 6

You open 1 ♡ with this hand and your partner bids 3 ♣. This is most delightful, of course, but still you should bid only 3 ♡. A jump to 4 ♡ would show a solid suit.

It may seem wrong to make the same bid with a strong hand as you would have made with a minimum opening, but you should remember that the bidding is bound to continue until game is reached. Here, of course, you have no intention of stopping below a small slam now that partner has forced. Because you have such excellent values, it is likely that your partner has little or nothing in reserve; probably he plans to limit his hand and let you take over. That will be the time for you to reassess the strength of your hand and decide just how far you want to go. For the moment, you simply define the *character* of your hand rather than its strength.

It is quite common for opener to rebid a useful five-card suit over a force when over a simple bid he would have introduced a new suit.

♠ A 4   ♡ 9 8   ◇ A K J 10 4   ♣ Q 10 6 3

You open 1 ◇ with this hand and partner bids 2 ♡. Rather than bid 3 ♣, it is better to rebid 3 ◇. If you are to reach a slam with this hand, diamonds are a much more likely trump suit than clubs.

RAISE OF RESPONDER'S SUIT

When the choice is between raising responder's suit and bidding a new suit, opener tends to bid as he would have done over a simple response. He should avoid the common mistake of raising responder's suit prematurely.

♠ K J 7 3   ♡ 5 4   ◇ K Q 3   ♣ A J 9 5

If the auction starts with 1 ♣-2 ◇, opener should rebid 2 ♠ with this hand, just as he would rebid 1 ♠ after 1 ♣-1 ◇. It is true that the responder may well have a five-card or six-card diamond suit, for which K-Q-x will represent magnificent support. But it is also possible that the responder has four spades and only four diamonds. In that case it will be hard to play in spades if diamonds are raised now. Furthermore, the spade bid is a step in describing where opener's values lie; it will always be possible to show diamond support, but if opener bids 3 ◇ now he will not be able to show strength in spades, for a subsequent bid in this suit will be a cue bid.

When opener raises responder's suit he does not have to bid the full value of his hand, as he would over a simple response. A single raise can now be made on a wide range of strength. After 1 ♣-2 ♠, you would raise to 3 ♠ with each of these hands.

(1) ♠ Q 7 4 3   ♡ Q 5   ◊ K Q 6   ♣ K Q 9 6
(2) ♠ A J 10 2   ♡ K Q   ◊ 9 3   ♣ A Q 10 8 3

Having raised with the first hand, you intend of course to do your best to keep partner on a short chain, but the immediate raise is still the right move. With (2) you raise in order to set the suit for a slam investigation; unless there are two losers in the red suits, the final contract will not be less than 6 ♠.

A jump raise of responder's suit shows excellent trump support and, once again, there is an inference that the hand contains little else of note.

♠ K Q 9 5   ♡ J 3   ◊ A Q 5 4 2   ♣ 7 5

After 1 ◊ -2 ♠, opener should jump to 4 ♠, showing limited high-card values but good support. This jump bid may be a helpful move if responder's main worry is about the trump suit.

OPENER BIDS A NEW SUIT

A bid of a new suit by opener is natural and unlimited. There is some difference of opinion concerning the meaning of "reverse" sequences such as the following:

(1)	OPENER	RESPONDER		(2)	OPENER	RESPONDER
	1 ♡	3 ♣			1 ♣	2 ♠
	3 ♠				3 ♡	

Some players take the position that these rebids should mean the same as over a simple response: at least 5-4 in the two suits and a minimum of 17 points. Others consider that a "reverse" over a force should show the distributional pattern, but not necessarily the high-card values, of a normal reverse bid. The important thing is to know how your partner treats these situations.

RESPONDER'S REBIDS AFTER A JUMP SHIFT

Two precepts should guide the rebid by a responder who has forced on the previous round. The first is that he should *beware of bidding the same values twice.*

OPENER	RESPONDER
1 ◇	2 ♠
3 ♣	?

Responder holds:

♠ A J 10 9 3   ♡ K Q 4   ◇ A 2   ♣ Q 8 3

The disciplined player bids 3 NT at this point, limiting his hand. If this call is passed, it will surely be the best contract. Any stronger call, such as 4 NT, should be avoided for responder has only the values he has already shown. Even a bid of 3 ♠ is poor, for it fails to bring the hand into the sharpest focus and may create unnecessary difficulties for opener.

This leads to the second precept: *The responder, unless he intends to take control, should try hard to identify the type of hand on which his force was based.* If he has a powerful fit for opener's first suit, he can now make this clear by giving support. If the force was based on an independent suit, responder can show this by rebidding it at his second turn. Note that the requirements for a rebiddable suit are now much more exacting than in a normal constructive auction—it will seldom be necessary for a responder to rebid a suit that is less sturdy than A-Q-10-x-x-x.

A fine point arises concerning the bid of a *new* suit by the responder after an original jump shift. There is no ambiguity if the auction is still at the 3-level:

OPENER	RESPONDER
1 ♡	3 ♣
3 ♡	3 ♠

This sequence is natural, showing longer clubs than spades
But take the case where the second suit is bid at the 4-level:

	OPENER	RESPONDER
	1 ♡	2 ♠
	3 ♡	4 ♣

We saw earlier that with a genuine two-suited hand the responder often develops the bidding slowly so as to be able to mention
both suits below the level of 3 NT. The bid of a new suit at the
4-level, as in this sequence, is therefore best treated as agreeing to
opener's suit. Thus 4 ♣ here would agree to hearts and show ♣ A.
This treatment is recommended because otherwise a hand like the
following can be hard to bid.

OPENER	RESPONDER
♠ K 4	♠ A Q J 8 2
♡ A Q 8 6 3 2	♡ K J 5
◇ K 10 4	◇ 7 3
♣ 10 3	♣ A K 5

OPENER	RESPONDER
1 ♡	2 ♠
3 ♡	?

If the responder were to bid 4 ♡ at this point, his partner, with
minimum values and no reassurance about the club suit, would have
to pass—and a slam would be missed. This raise does not really do
justice to the responder's hand. At the same time, he does not want
to take control by bidding 4 NT, for if opener has only one ace it
will not be clear whether there are two diamond losers. A bid of
4 ♣, if understood as a cue bid, provides a solution: Opener now
knows that he is facing a hand of this strength and, with second-
round control of diamonds and the key ♠ K, should bid 4 NT,
planning to continue to 6 ♡.

MISFIT HANDS

Even the best of partnerships can get to bad contracts when the cards fit badly. On some deals each hand looks highly promising in isolation, but the players have voids and singletons in each other's suit and the final contract proves a death trap. Therefore it is necessary to bid cautiously when the bidding provides evidence of a positive misfit. Do not assume that game will be safe on 26 or 27 points, or that the success of a small slam will be assured with 33 or 34. These figures apply to hands that fit normally. Just as you may reduce them when there is evidence of an excellent fit, so you must increase the figures when there is a misfit.

The duty of recognizing a misfit rests very largely with the responder, who on the second round may spot the discouraging symptoms. The bidding goes:

OPENER	RESPONDER
1 ♡	2 ♠
3 ◇	?

Responder holds:

♠ A K J 7 5 4   ♡ 6   ◇ 10 7 2   ♣ A K Q

Opener may have a useful, not too unbalanced hand, say 5-4-2-2, making 6 NT playable. Or he may have opened on a shapely sub-minimum hand such as this:

♠ —   ♡ K Q 9 5 3   ◇ A J 8 6 3   ♣ J 10 7

Responder should bid 3 NT at this point, taking the more cautious view. It is tempting to rebid 3 ♠, but then there will be no way of staying within range of 3 NT, for it is clear that opener will not be able to bid 3 NT from his side of the table for lack of a club guard. Now, over 3 NT, opener too must be alert to the danger of a misfit: to take out into 4 ◇ with the hand above would be very bad.

Quiz on Developing the Bidding After a Jump Shift

You open 1 ◇ and your partner bids 2 ♠. What is your rebid with each of the following hands?

(1) ♠ 7 3   ♡ K 8 5   ◇ A K Q J 8 6 4   ♣ 2
(2) ♠ Q 3   ♡ A 5   ◇ K Q J 10 8   ♣ K 7 6 2
(3) ♠ K Q 7 3   ♡ 8 2   ◇ A K J 8 4   ♣ 10 4
(4) ♠ K 4   ♡ A 10 6   ◇ K J 8 7 3   ♣ A 10 8
(5) ♠ K J 8   ♡ 7 3   ◇ K Q 6 4 2   ♣ Q J 5

Your partner opens 1 ♡ and rebids 3 ♡ over your response of 2 ♠. What do you bid now on the following hands?

(6) ♠ A Q 9 8 5   ♡ Q 3   ◇ K J 4   ♣ K Q 3
(7) ♠ A Q J 9 8 3   ♡ 7 5   ◇ 10 3   ♣ A Q 4
(8) ♠ A Q 7 5 2   ♡ Q 4 3   ◇ A K 4   ♣ J 7
(9) ♠ A K Q J 7 5 2   ♡ J   ◇ K J 3   ♣ J 4
(10) ♠ A K J 10 7   ♡ K 10 8   ◇ A K 4   ♣ J 7

Solutions

1. 4 ◇. This jump rebid in a forcing situation shows a solid suit with at least six-card length. It does not necessarily imply extra values.
2. 3 ◇. The chances of a slam seem quite high, and your first concern should be to locate a satisfactory trump suit. It is therefore inadvisable to introduce this sketchy club

suit. A bid of 2 NT would be unconstructive, for it is most unlikely that partner will be able to support diamonds unless you rebid the suit now.

3. 4 ♠. This jump raise shows generous four-card trump support and not much more than minimum high-card values, with probably no controls in the unbid suits.

4. 2 NT. A slam is likely here, as you have sound strength and excellent controls. The important thing is to ensure playing in the right denomination. The 2 NT bid allows partner to rebid his spade suit or show support for diamonds; in either case you would be home free. And if partner simply bids 3 NT, you will still raise to 4 NT.

5. 3 ♠. This single raise is the same rebid that you would have made over a simple response, but you should bear in mind that partner will not immediately know that it is based on a minimum opening. If partner continues with a slam try you should express, initially at any rate, a total lack of enthusiasm.

6. 3 NT. This rebid shows that your jump shift was based on general values and that you hold nothing much in the way of undisclosed values. Any move toward slam will have to come from your partner.

7. 3 ♠. Once again this is the most descriptive move, showing that your force was based on a good, but probably not solid, suit.

8. 4 ♡. Now that partner has rebid his suit, your Q-x-x constitutes excellent support. However, no stronger action is justified as you have no more than a minimum force. To cue-bid 4 ◇ would represent an overstatement; to go to 4 NT would be a serious blunder.

9. 4 ♠. This jump rebid shows a solid suit, playable in slam opposite a void. Furthermore, as the jump rebid is at game level and may be passed, there is an inference that no other very noteworthy features are held.

10. 4 ◇. A raise to 4 ♡ would be too cautious: There will surely be a play for 6 ♡ if opener can control the club suit. Unless you cue-bid 4 ◇ at this point, agreeing on hearts and showing first-round control of diamonds, it will be hard to reach 6 ♡ if opener's hand is, say:

♠ Q x   ♡ A Q J x x   ◇ J x x   ♣ K 10 x

Other Strong Responses to a One-Bid

A double raise of opener's suit, which increasingly is treated in the modern game as non-forcing, is covered in the next chapter. The remaining strong responses to a one-bid are the bids of 2 NT and 3 NT.

THE 2 NT RESPONSE TO 1 ♣,1 ♢ , 1 ♡, 1 ♠

The response of 2 NT has been labeled a "slam killer." It need not be so if the values shown are precise and the rebid sequences are clearly understood.

An immediate response of 2 NT to an opening suit bid of one is game-forcing and shows a balanced hand with 13-15 points. It relieves the responder of the embarrassment of having to bid a weak suit with such a hand as this:

♠ Q 7 2   ♡ A J 5   ♢ A Q J   ♣ J 9 6 4

After an opening bid of 1 ♠, the forcing response of 2 NT describes this hand well. The 2 NT response is restricted to hands of 4-3-3-3 distribution or 4-4-3-2 with the doubleton in the opener's suit. Unless the hand is completely balanced, 2 NT tends to deny a biddable four-card major that could have been shown at the one-level.

The player who responds with 2 NT is suggesting that the final contract should be 3 NT, and opener is likely to accept this suggestion unless his hand contains a singleton or he is interested in slam. In either case, opener will most often proceed by way of an exploratory bid at the 3-level. Some examples follow.

(1)	OPENER	RESPONDER
♠	A 2	♠ K 8 4
♡	K J 7 6 3 2	♡ A Q 5
♢	A Q 4 3	♢ K 10 2
♣	9	♣ Q 8 4 3

OPENER	RESPONDER
1 ♡	2 NT
3 ◊ (a)	4 ♡ (b)
4 NT	5 ◊
6 ♡	Pass

(a) Opener could go straight to 4 ♡ over 2 NT but there is a possibility of slam if responder has the right cards.

(b) As the majority of his points are in opener's suits, responder makes an encouraging noise—here his jump-preference rebid enables opener to bid slam. A bid of 3 ♡ would simply indicate three-card heart support without any encouragement.

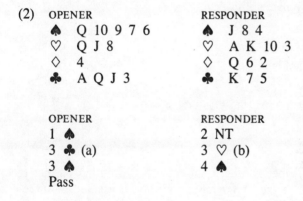

(2)	OPENER	RESPONDER
♠	Q 10 9 7 6	J 8 4
♡	Q J 8	A K 10 3
◊	4	Q 6 2
♣	A Q J 3	K 7 5

OPENER	RESPONDER
1 ♠	2 NT
3 ♣ (a)	3 ♡ (b)
3 ♠	4 ♠
Pass	

With this very common type of hand it is all too easy to reach the wrong game contract. After a forcing 2 NT response, care is needed to get to 4 ♠.

(a) From opener's angle, 3 NT may well be the best contract if responder has strength in diamonds. Responder is expected to avoid raising this secondary minor suit, which may conceivably be only three cards.

(b) This too may be a three-card suit; responder is simply showing a strong holding. If this suit was opener's weakness, opener would bid 3 NT. As it is, opener expresses a further preference for the spade game, and with three-card support the responder raises.

THE 3 NT RESPONSE TO 1 ♣, 1 ◊, 1 ♡ OR 1 ♠

This bid shows 16-18 points with, of course, a sure guard in each suit and, specifically, a 4-3-3-3 distribution. This is in line with the principle that any response which carries the bidding to a high level should be precisely defined, as little space is left for exploration. Used on other hand patterns, the 3 NT response truly is a slam killer.

After a 3 NT response, opener is faced with the straightforward question of whether his hand merits a slam effort. Suppose that the bidding goes:

OPENER	RESPONDER
1 ♠	3 NT
?	

Opener holds:

(1) ♠ K Q 9 4 3   ♡ Q J 7   ◊ A 8 2   ♣ K 9
(2) ♠ K 10 7 4 3 2   ♡ 6   ◊ K 10 2   ♣ A K 5

With (1) opener bids a natural 4 NT, inviting partner to bid 6 NT if he is in the upper range. With (2), assured of three-card spade support, opener can assume that the values for 6 ♠ are present, for to his existing 15 points he may now add two points for shortness. He has to check on aces, however; a direct 4 NT would be quantitative, so he first bids 4 ♣. Now, over any response from partner, 4 NT will ask for aces.

Powerhouse Rebids by Opener

The jump-shift rebid by the opener has an important place in the scheme of things. It covers hands where the opener, after his partner's simple response in a new suit, intends to reach game, and especially those hands where he is as yet unsure of the best denomination. It consists of a *single* jump in a new suit, as in these sequences:

(1) OPENER   RESPONDER   (2) OPENER   RESPONDER
     1 ♣   1 ♡   1 ♡   1 ♠
     2 ♠   3 ♣

Inasmuch as the responder may have no more than about 6 points, these rebids by opener necessarily show at least 20 points. There are three types of strong opening hand that may qualify for this treatment.

1. Hands containing about 20 high-card points. When you open 1 ♣, 1 ◇, 1 ♡ or 1 ♠ with a hand as strong as this, and your partner responds, you *must* ensure that game is reached. Often a hand of this type will be relatively balanced (for otherwise it would probably have justified a stronger opening) and may therefore be suitable for a rebid of 3 NT. But opener does not normally rebid at 3 NT if this means concealing a four-card major suit.

                    OPENER   RESPONDER
                    1 ◇   1 ♡
                     ?

Opener holds:

(1) ♠ A Q 8 2   ♡ J 4   ◇ A K Q 5   ♣ A 7 4
(2) ♠ K J 3   ♡ Q 7   ◇ A K J 2   ♣ K Q J 4

With (1) the rebid is 2 ♠, for if responder has four cards in this suit as well as in hearts, a contract of 4 ♠ will very probably be best. With (2) opener jumps to 3 NT on the second round.

2. Two-suited hands containing at least 20 points including distribution. Players who do not employ Intermediate Twos quite often have to open at one of a suit with a two-suited hand that falls just short of a 2 ♣ opening. With this type hand it may be advisable to force on the second round even if partner's response is in an unfavorable suit. For example:

OPENER	RESPONDER
1 ♡	1 ♠
3 ◇	

Opener holds:

♠ 7   ♡ K Q J 7 4   ◇ A K Q 8 3   ♣ K 6

It would be wrong to rebid 2 ◇ with this very powerful hand; first because this might be passed, and secondly because opener might find it impossible to "catch up" after making this colossal underbid.

When the responder has bid 1 NT, it is useful to have the understanding that a jump shift by opener is forcing for only one round. It then becomes possible for opener to cope fluently with a wide range of two-suited hands. The bidding goes:

OPENER	RESPONDER
1 ♠	1 NT
?	

Opener holds:

♠ A K 10 4 3   ♡ K J 7 4   ◇ A Q 3   ♣ 8

This hand is hard to bid accurately unless a jump to 3 ♡ is treated as a one-round force. Opener is prepared to bid game if partner has four hearts, but he intends to pass a simple bid of 3 ♠. Responder, therefore, must jump to 4 ♠ if he has secondary support for spades and one or two useful cards. He bids 3 NT only if his hand is maximum in terms of points, with no support for opener's suits.

3. Hands that have been improved by partner's response.
Before the advent of the "fragment" bid (see next chapter), a jump-shift rebid by opener was often based on a hand that had gained in stature as a result of a very favorable response. Suppose that you open 1 ◊ and partner bids 1 ♠. You hold:

♠ K J 9 4　　♡ 2　　◊ A K J 7 3　　♣ A J 10

This hand contains only 17 points in high cards, but a rebid of 3 ♣, to be followed by a game bid in spades, is the only way to do justice to the excellent fit with partner.

Playing "fragment" bids, this hand would be shown by a rebid of 4 ♣. But a jump shift rebid may still be based partly on a fit in responder's suit when opener has this type of hand:

♠ K Q 2　　♡ A Q 10 6 4　　◊ A K 4　　♣ 10 2

You open 1 ♡ and partner bids 1 ♠. It is still possible there may be no game anywhere in the hand, but your hand is so improved by partner's response that a game-forcing bid of 3 ◊ is a reasonable speculation. If partner has either five spades or three hearts, game is likely to be there. If he has not, he may be able to bid 3 NT. It will be noted that although 3 ◊ is an overbid, it at least ensures that the hand will be played in the right denomination. The same cannot be said of any alternative move.

Quiz on Opener's Powerhouse Rebids

You open 1 ◊ and your partner responds 1 ♡. What is your rebid with each of the following hands?

(1) ♠ A Q J 10　♡ Q 2　◊ A K Q 10 2　♣ J 3
(2) ♠ Q 10 7 4　♡ K 9 2　◊ A K Q 5 4　♣ A

(3) ♠ K 4 ♡ A J 6 ◊ K Q 10 5 ♣ A Q J 10
(4) ♠ Q 7 2 ♡ A 6 ◊ A K Q 10 4 3 ♣ K 4
(5) ♠ A K 6 3 ♡ K J 8 ◊ A K 3 2 ♣ K 4

Solutions

1. 2 ♠. Now that partner has bid hearts, you may attach value to the doubleton queen of this suit. This brings your hand to 20 points, and you should not be willing to risk being passed out at 1 ♠.

2. 1 ♠. You need a further bid from partner before you can be sure of game—either a rebid in hearts, support for spades or a voluntary bid of notrump.

3. 3 NT. A bid of 3 ♣ is a reasonable second choice, but in the long haul it will pay to bid this hand as the balanced powerhouse that it is.

4. 3 NT. With a nearly solid six-card suit, this hand is the equal of many hands that are two or three points stronger in high cards.

5. 2 ♠. With so many high cards you must be sure of reaching game. Partner's next bid will show whether this is to be at hearts, spades or notrump.

4

The Big Trump Fit

♠ ♡ ◇ ♣

Valuing Your Hand—Raises and Rebids in the Trump Suit—"Fragment" Bids and "Splinter" Bids—The Poor Man's Ace—Trump Solidity— The Grand Slam Force—The Swiss Convention —The Losing Trick Count

In some number of hands your partner will desist from his usual exasperating habit of bidding suits that you are short on and withholding support for suits that you are long on. When this happens a mutually satisfactory trump suit may be brought to light, causing your hand to blossom like a rose. Then it becomes vital to have an accurate way of measuring how much more your hand is worth.

Before attending to this pleasant theme, it is well to note that there is actually some skill in deciding what *constitutes* a big trump fit. In other words, what are the signs that cause you to decide, irrevocably, that the hand should be played with this suit as trump? There are certain very reliable indicators.

With nine or more cards in a major suit you should virtually always play with this suit as trump. Once in a blue moon you may elect to play 3 NT with a solid major suit divided 6-3 between the two hands, but the trump contract should invariably be preferred when this suit is divided 5-4, even when the other features of the hand appear to favor a notrump contract.

71

```
          YOU        PARTNER
          1 ♠        3 ♠
           ?
```

You hold:

♠ K J 7 4 2   ♡ A Q   ◇ K 10 4   ♣ Q 10 6

It is tempting to bid 3 NT, but this is unlikely to be the best contract, for there will surely be a weakness in one of the side suits despite the strength of your holdings. Unless you and your partner have agreed to play five-card major-suit openings, you can assume in this sequence that there will be nine trumps in the combined hands, as partner will not jump-raise you on three. Accordingly, you should bid 4 ♠.

With eight cards in a major suit divided 4-4, it is still right to play in the suit unless both hands are balanced. Therefore when the opening bid is 1 ♡ or 1 ♠ and you have four-card support for the suit, you should raise, even with a 4-3-3-3 pattern, as it is quite unlikely that your partner also has this pattern. In any case, if the opener is fairly balanced he will not go to game in the major suit without first exploring the possibility of notrump.

It is a different matter when the opening bid is 1 NT. Now, if your hand is perfectly balanced, you do not normally make a Stayman bid of 2 ♣ in search of a 4-4 fit, as you assume that your partner also is balanced. When you have a 4-4-3-2 pattern, however, you must consult your judgment: Generally it will be right to play in a 4-4 major suit unless your support for this suit is very weak and you have reason to think that game will be safer in notrump.

Later in this chapter it will be seen that the advantages of a 4-4 fit have to weighed with still more deliberation when a slam contract is under consideration.

With eight cards divided 5-3, the benefit of a trump contract is not quite so great. When you have a 4-4 fit you may hope to draw the opponents' trumps and still have a trump left in each hand—a great advantage. With a 5-3 fit this is not possible.

In general, therefore, you tend to play in the trump contract only when there is a weakness in one or more side suits or when the short trump hand has a ruffing potential. In the following sequence your partner has shown a five-card heart suit.

	YOU	PARTNER
	1 ♠	2 ♡
	3 ♡	3 NT
	?	

You hold:

(1) ♠ K Q 5 3 2   ♡ A 7 4   ◇ Q J 8 3   ♣ 7
(2) ♠ A 9 8 7 4   ♡ K 8 2   ◇ K J   ♣ Q 8 6

With (1) you should put partner into 4 ♡, as your hand is likely to produce one or two club ruffs. With (2) you pass 3 NT, as there is no reason to think that any suit is wide open or that your hand is very likely to produce a ruffing trick. You do not expect to be right every time in these decisions, but nevertheless you must *decide*, rather than go by hard-and-fast rules. Again:

	PARTNER	YOU
	1 ♠	2 ♣
	2 NT	?

You hold:

♠ Q 9 3   ♡ K Q   ◇ Q J 2   ♣ Q J 8 4 2

The normal move with this type of responding hand is to bid 3 ♠, forcing, giving partner the option of 4 ♠ or 3 NT. Here, however, you can see that your hand is unlikely to provide a ruffing trick in hearts, as opener is likely to have either the ace or J-10-x-x. The recommended bid is therefore 3 NT. (Why is 3 ♠ forcing? Because a response of 2 ♣ or 2 ◇ shows at least 10 points and more often 11. Thus when opener has made the strength-showing rebid of 2 NT, responder will never want to stop at three of a major in this sequence.)

Strangely enough, with a 5-3 trump suit it is more likely that you should play in a trump contract *when this suit is ragged* than when it is solid. This is because you may never have time to establish a ragged suit if you play at notrump. With the hands below, the choice is between 3 NT and game in spades.

	PARTNER	YOU
	1 ♣	1 ♠
	2 ♠	?

You hold:

(1) ♠ A Q 10 8 3   ♡ K 7   ◇ Q 10 4   ♣ K 10 2
(2) ♠ J 8 7 4 2   ♡ A K 3   ◇ A K 5   ♣ 10 6

In each case you assume that you have only a 5-3 spade fit. (If your partner has four spades, he will insist that you play in this suit no matter what you bid at this point.) With (1) there is an excellent chance that your spade suit and your partner's club suit will provide nine running tricks, so the right bid is 3 NT. With (2) it is likely that there will be work to do before the black suits become established. At 4 ♠ you will have more control than at 3 NT, and in addition you may expect partner to have a ruffing value in one of the red suits.

What has been said so far applies to major-suit contracts. Game in a minor suit is generally avoided, even when a big trump fit is present, unless it is clear that game in notrump will be endangered by extreme weakness in one or more side suits.

Valuing Your Hand

When you have found a good trump suit, the next step is to consider how much your hand is worth with this suit as trump. The importance of a sound method of valuation cannot be overstated.

The majority of failures in high trump contracts stem from the failure of one partner or the other to value his hand accurately.

The author's favorite method of valuation is the Losing Trick Count, but this has been relegated to the end of the chapter out of consideration for the fact that it is not the most popular. Incidentally, there is nothing against using *two* methods of valuation; when you have a big decision, such as whether to try for a slam, it can be useful to have this doublecheck, for no single method of valuation is entirely reliable.

The most widely used method is *combined point count*. In one popular version you start by counting the high-card points in the usual way, 4-3-2-1 for aces, kings, queens and jacks. Next you add one point for the fifth card in any suit, one point for the sixth card and two points for each subsequent card. Finally, when you have a satisfactory trump suit, you add "support" points: 3 for a void, 2 for a singleton, 1 for a doubleton.

This method can be used both when raising your partner's suit and when revaluing after you have been raised by partner. And of course the usual vital statistics apply: 26 points for game in a major suit, 29 for game in a minor, 33 or 34 for slam. In this example, after a routine initial response, the use of point count gives the responder a clear indication of the final contract.

OPENER	RESPONDER
♠ A 10 7	♠ K 6
♡ K Q 10 8	♡ A 9 7 3 2
◇ K J 10	◇ A 6 3
♣ 9 8 6	♣ A K 4

OPENER	RESPONDER
1 ♡	3 ♣
3 NT	6 ♡
Pass	

Opener's 3 NT rebid suggests no more than minimum values, so the responder may bank on no more than 13 points. Responder, however, has 18 points in high cards, plus one for length and one for the spade shortage. In addition, you should always take an optimistic view when there are nine trumps in the combined hands. This

means the slam should be fairly safe, so responder goes straight to
6 ♡. Note that the slam is in fact icy: Declarer draws trumps (in
three rounds if necessary), ruffs a spade and exits with A-K and
another club, forcing a diamond return or a ruff and discard. It is the
presence of the ninth trump that makes this such a strong line of
play.

Now suppose you are the responder in this sequence:

OPENER	RESPONDER
1 ♣	1 ♠
3 ♠	?

Responder holds:

♠ Q J 10 4   ♡ A 9 3   ◇ 8 6   ♣ J 8 5 2

Opener's jump raise suggests 17-19 points. You started out
with only 8 points, but now that the spades have been supported you
may add a point for the doubleton diamond. With the assurance of at
least 26 points in the two hands, you are worth a bid of 4 ♠.

In the next example you are the opening bidder:

YOU	PARTNER
1 ♣	1 ♡
1 ♠	3 ♠
?	

You hold:

♠ A Q 8 3   ♡ Q 6 4   ◇ 10 4   ♣ K J 10 4

You started out with a minimum hand—and you still have only

13 points, even after your partner's jump raise. There are no redeeming features, such as an extra trump, so you simply pass.

This method of valuation is subject to all the usual adjustments.
Unguarded honor cards are demoted, high cards in partner's suit are
promoted. Moreover, high cards in any long suit are looked upon
more favorably than those in a short suit, for in addition to their
normal high-card value they will help promote the long cards. In
close situations you should also take account of the fact that aces are
slightly undervalued in the 4-3-2-1 count, and that queens and jacks
are overvalued.

When you are hoping to gain several ruffers in your hand, low
trumps may be more productive than high ones. Suppose the opening bid is 1 ♠ and the responder has these hands, each containing
10 high-card points.

(1) ♠ A K Q 3   ♡ J 10 7 4 3   ◇ 10 7 4 2   ♣ —
(2) ♠ 10 8 4 3   ♡ J 10 7 4 3   ◇ A K Q 2   ♣ —

Both hands may reasonably be expected to make game in
spades, but the second is probably the better hand because declarer
may make several club ruffs as well as A-K-Q of diamonds. Thus
while with (1) you would raise straight to 4 ♠, expressing the only
real feature of your hand, with (2) it would be reasonable to respond
first with 2 ◇, intending to raise to 4 ♠ on the next round. This is a
stronger sequence, of course. How accurately you express such
hands as these will frequently mean the difference between getting
too high and missing a slam.

When it is a question of getting to game, I recommend that you
add one point to your hand when you can count on nine or ten
trumps in the combined hands. This is because a declarer who has
no worries about the trump suit is in a stronger position than one
who has to cope with a tenuous 4-4 or 5-3 holding: He has more
tactical plans at his command—suit establishment, eliminations and
so on. I also recommend that you add still another point when a
long, ragged suit has been supported. Suppose you are the responder
and the bidding goes:

PARTNER   YOU
1 ♣   1 ♠
2 ♠   ?

You hold:

♠ K 10 7 4 3 2   ♡ A 10 6   ◇ 5 3   ♣ 10 3

Initially this hand was worth 9 points. Now that the spades have been raised, you may add 2 for shortness, but this still does not fully reflect the enrichment that occurs when a broken six-card suit is supported. If partner has a bare minimum there may be no more than 24 points in the two hands; nevertheless, you should try for game by bidding 3 ♠. It would not be a bad gamble to go straight to game! When you get to the stage of making this kind of assessment, you are no longer relying very much upon point count but upon your own judgment, and this indeed is what you should aim at.

Raises and Rebids in the Trump Suit

It is possible to set out the points required for every raise and rebid in an agreed trump suit. Thus when supporting opener's suit you raise from one to two with 6-9 points, from one to three with 10-12 points. (This is assuming limit raises, as described later. If the double raise is a game force, responder must find a one-round force at his first turn and give the raise to the 3-level subsequently.) With 13 points or more, you intend to reach game one way or another.

The same principle can be followed by the opening hand and also by responder when raising opener's second suit. Thus:

OPENER   RESPONDER
1 ♣   1 ♡
1 ♠   ?

Responder holds:

(1) ♠ Q 10 8 3   ♡ A Q 7 4 2   ◇ 6   ♣ 9 8 4
(2) ♠ A J 7 2   ♡ K Q 10 7 3   ◇ 9 3   ♣ 10 2

Hand (1) was initially worth 9 points but is now worth 11 in support of spades. Responder therefore raises to 3 ♠, a limit bid. With (2), which is now worth 13 points, he raises to 4 ♠.

We now take a more detailed look at the main raises and rebids that occur in a powerhouse auction.

THE LIMIT DOUBLE RAISE

The raise from one to three in opener's major suit is one of the most effective moves in bridge, for it so often shuts out the opponents. In order to make full use of this bid, most leading players now play *limit* double raises: Virtually all hands in the 10-12 point range with four-card support for opener's major suit are described by an immediate double raise, which is not forcing. Your partner opens 1 ♡ and you hold:

(1) ♠ 7   ♡ K J 8 3   ◇ A 9 7 4   ♣ 10 8 6 3
(2) ♠ K 9 7 4 2   ♡ Q 9 6 3   ◇ 10 2   ♣ A 4

With each of these hands you go straight to 3 ♡. With (1), worth 10 points, you may succeed in shutting out a spade contract. With (2), worth 12 points, there is no advantage in bidding 1 ♠ on the first round, as this may allow the opponents to compete in the minor suits. It is unlikely that there can be any better contract than hearts.

A double raise in a minor suit has a slightly higher upper limit because it is so important to stay within range of 3 NT. (In addition, of course, you do not raise a minor suit until you have considered the chances of finding a fit in a major.) Your partner opens 1 ◇ and you hold:

♠ A 10 7   ♡ 4 2   ◇ A Q J 3   ♣ J 10 6 3

This hand is worth at least 13 points in support of diamonds. (It includes two aces, which tend to be undervalued.) Nevertheless, a raise to 3 ◇ is best. If this were a major suit you would not dream of making such an underbid: You would either make use of the Swiss Convention* or bid 2 ♣ on the first round and raise to game on the next.

THE FORCING DOUBLE RAISE

The more traditional meaning of the double raise, still widely used, is to show strong support with the equivalent of opening values, 13-15 points. This bid is forcing to game. The following would be a typical hand for a raise of 1 ♡ to 3 ♡, or 1 ♠ to 3 ♠.

♠ A Q 10 7   ♡ Q J 9 2   ◇ A 7 3   ♣ 10 8

Some players who employ the forcing double raise in an uncontested auction revert to the limit raise when there is intervention by second hand. And a double raise by a passed hand is *always* a limit raise.

THE TRIPLE RAISE

The raise from one to four in opener's suit is based mainly on distribution. It shows at least 13 points, of which no more than about 9 are in high cards. Your partner opens 1 ♠ and you hold:

♠ Q 9 8 6 3   ♡ 7   ◇ A 10 8 5 4 2   ♣ 4

Despite its weakness in high cards, this hand is worth 13 points in support of spades. You should raise straight to game.

*See page 93.

OPENER'S REBID

Point count can be helpful all the way through the bidding process. When the responder has bid at the one level, he may have no more than 6 points. Opener therefore needs 20 points to raise the responder's major suit to the level of game. For a double raise he needs 17-19 points. With less he is normally worth only a single raise, although some 16-point hands may be treated as exceptions. Thus:

	OPENER	RESPONDER
	1 ♣	1 ♠
	?	

Opener holds:

(1) ♠ A K J 2   ♡ 10 8 4   ◇ 9 2   ♣ A Q 7 3
(2) ♠ A 8 7 2   ♡ 7   ◇ A 6 2   ♣ A J 8 4 2
(3) ♠ K Q J 4   ♡ A 4   ◇ 10 7   ♣ A Q J 7 3

In the first hand opener has exceptional trump support, but with 15 points he should raise only to 2 ♠. Hand (2) is worth 16 points. Because it contains three aces, a raise to 3 ♠ is justified. Hand (3), with 20 points, is worth a raise to 4 ♠.

When the responder has bid at the 2-level, the same principles may be applied with some adjustments, based on the fact that the responder's minimum is now 10 points. It is also necessary to be more flexible because there is less space in which to operate. Consider this auction:

	OPENER	RESPONDER
	1 ♠	2 ♡
	?	

Opener holds:

(1) ♠ A Q 8 7 2   ♡ A 10 4   ◇ 9 7   ♣ K Q 5
(2) ♠ A K 10 4 3   ♡ J 9 6   ◇ A 7 2   ♣ 4 2

In (1) opener has 16 points and responder is expected to have 10. Opener has only three-card support for his partner's known five-card suit, but against this can be balanced the fact that he has two aces. He therefore has enough for a raise to 4 ♡. Some players underbid in this situation, arguing that any raise to the 3-level shows above-minimum values. A raise to only 3 ♡, however, goes against the principle that you should bid what you think you can make. Moreover, the opener should be left free to raise to 3 ♡ with an appreciably weaker hand than this, provided it belongs indubitably in hearts.

Thus with (2) opener should raise to 3 ♡ despite having only 13 points. For opener stolidly to rebid his own suit here would invite the disaster of going down in 2 ♠—partner having a singleton —when perhaps even a game could be made in hearts.

TRIAL BIDS

A player with a fair hand, whose opening bid of 1 ♡ or 1 ♠ is raised to two, often wants to make a noncommittal try for game in this suit. The recognized way of doing so is by means of a trial bid in a new suit.

OPENER	RESPONDER
1 ♠	2 ♠
3 ◇	

Here 3 ◇ is a trial bid, with spades agreed as trump. The trial bid indicates where opener most needs assistance: an "empty" four-card suit such as A-x-x-x, for instance. The following would be a typical hand:

♠ Q J 9 4 3   ♡ A K J   ◇ A 7 4 3   ♣ 5

Opener started out with 16 points and, adding two for shortness now that his suit has been supported, he should try for game opposite partner's 6-9 points. To bid simply 3 ♠ would be a crude method of exploration. A trial bid of 3 ◇ will enable the responder to value his hand very much more accurately, as can be seen from these examples:

(1) ♠ K 8 6 2   ♡ 10 7 4   ◇ K 2   ♣ J 8 4 3
(2) ♠ Q 8 7 5   ♡ Q 4   ◇ 6 5 2   ♣ Q J 6 4
(3) ♠ A 10 8 2   ♡ 8 4   ◇ 9 8 6   ♣ A 10 7 2

With (1) responder bids a confident 4 ♠, for although he has minimal values, both his kings are "working" and the diamond holding is ideal. With (2) he signs off in 3 ♠—he has fair values, but these are in all the wrong places. With (3) he has a very poor diamond holding, but his hand is excellent in other respects. So he still bids 4♠. It is not merely that he has 2 points more than the minimum requirement; he has two aces, which are certain to be useful, whereas second- and third-round points may never come into play.

The technique of the trial bid is so extremely helpful that many players have altogether abandoned the constructive use of a bid of three in such a sequence as this:

OPENER	RESPONDER
1 ♠	2 ♠
3 ♠	

Opener's raise to three in this sequence is used not to show extra strength but to shut out the opponents with a hand such as this:

♠ A K 10 7 5 4   ♡ 3   ◇ Q J 6   ♣ Q 8 2

Some tournament players use what are called short suit trial bids: After a single raise, opener rebids in a short suit where help is *not* wanted.

THE JUMP SHIFT BY A PASSED HAND

Because it is common to open light in third or fourth position, there can be few occasions for a jump shift by a player who has passed unless he happens to hold good support for opener's suit. It is helpful, therefore, to have the understanding that a jump shift by a passed hand is a guarantee of good support for opener's suit, with the values for a raise to at least the three level. The advantage is that the opener may be able to jump to game with quite a modest hand when he has a good fit in the side suit. This is the sort of hand with which you would jump to 3 ◇ in response to a third- or fourth-hand opening of 1 ♠:

♠ A 10 7 2   ♡ 9 8 4   ◇ K 10 8 4 3   ♣ 7

This hand is worth a raise to 3 ♠, but a bid of 3 ◇, guaranteeing support for spades, is clearly more informative. With the hand below, opener would be emboldened by the good diamond fit to jump to game.

♠ Q 8 6 5 3   ♡ A 6   ◇ A Q 2   ♣ J 8 2

It follows that if opener can do no more than rebid his suit at the 3-level, responder may pass. Responder may also use this jump shift with a more powerful hand, worth a raise to game, as this may lead to a slam if opener is strong. Thus:

OPENER	RESPONDER
♠ A 7 2	♠ 8 4
♡ A Q 9 6 3	♡ K 10 8 5
◇ A 10 6	◇ 5 2
♣ K 2	♣ A Q 9 7 3

OPENER	RESPONDER
—	Pass
1 ♡	3 ♣ (a)
3 ◇ (b)	4 ♡
6 ♡	Pass

(a) Responder is worth a raise to 4 ♡. However, he selects the more informative bid of 3 ♣, intending to push on to 4 ♡ even if opener makes the weak rebid of 3 ♡.

(b) As it happens, opener is strong, with good controls and an excellent club fit. For the moment he temporizes, as he does not know whether responder is worth 3 ♡ or 4 ♡. When responder clarifies his hand on the next round, opener is able to bid the slam.

"Fragment" Bids and "Splinter" Bids

These are simple and effective devices that effect an improvement in an area where it is vitally needed—the slam zone. They are based on the sound idea of showing partner where your values are, and therefore have much to commend them. Suppose you are the opener with this hand:

♠ A 10 8 4   ♡ 2   ◇ A Q 7   ♣ A K 10 7 6

You open 1 ♣ and partner, to your pleasure, responds 1 ♠. A raise to 4 ♠ is justified, but this bid, although it announces a powerhouse, is not ideal as slam may depend on how well your values in the unbid suits are working. The two hands may be these:

OPENER	RESPONDER
♠ A 10 8 4	♠ K Q 7 5 2
♡ 2	♡ J 8 4
◇ A Q 7	◇ K 6 2
♣ A K 10 7 6	♣ 9 4

A 6 ♠ contract is almost icy, but if the bidding starts with
1 ♣-1 ♠-4 ♠, the responder is apt to meditate along these lines:
"Partner has shown 20 points and I have 11. We must have nine
trumps between us, so I may add a point. This still leaves us short
on a slam unless the hands are a perfect fit. I am not sure whether
my ♦ K is of any value, so I am not going to risk going down in
5 ♠ by making any kind of slam try." In general this would be
reasonable thinking, but here a slam would be missed as a result.

The purpose of the "fragment" bid is to highlight, in this type
of sequence, a significant feature in a third suit. With the hand
above, on the second round the opener jumps not to 4 ♠ but to
4 ♦, a bid that has no natural meaning. This says, "I have the
values for a raise to 4 ♠, with a useful feature in diamonds. I have
no more than a singleton in the remaining suit, hearts. I am thinking
about a possible slam if you have the right stuff in the right places,
and if your hand is a little better than a minimum."

A fragment bid, therefore, is defined as a double jump in a new
suit on the second round, showing big support for partner and a
singleton in the unbid suit. It consumes no more space than a natural
raise to game, and it is more informative. Here the responder should
feel encouraged to hie himself slamwards over 4 ♦, as he can see
that ♦ K is a useful card and that there are almost no wasted values
in hearts. The logical next step for responder in this instance is a
Blackwood checkback on aces to make sure that opener has the
needed three.

No less an advantage is that a fragment bid may avert an
unmakable slam. Consider the responding hand in this sequence:

OPENER	RESPONDER
1 ♡	1 ♠
4 ♣	?

Responder holds:

♠ A 10 9 8 4   ♡ 8 5 2   ◇ K Q 10 2   ♣ 4

With this hand the responder can detect and avoid the kind of
poor slam contract that we have all gone down in so often. He
reasons: "No doubt we have 32 or 33 points, but my values in

diamonds, where partner has a singleton, must be at least partially wasted. There is therefore bound to be a weakness elsewhere, probably in the vital heart suit.'' Here the responder should sign off in 4 ♠. With ◊ A instead of K-Q, he would bid 4 ◊.

Finally, a negative inference may arise when opener bypasses the use of a fragment bid.

OPENER   RESPONDER
1 ♣   1 ♠
4 ♠   ?

Responder holds:

♠ Q J 9 4 2   ♡ A 7 4 3   ◊ 6   ♣ Q 10 5

With this borderline hand the responder may say: ''As my partner evidently lacks the requirements for a fragment bid, he is likely to be unusually strong in the black suits. As I have the red suits under control, I am going to bid 4 NT and go on to slam if partner has two aces.'' It would not be right to cue-bid ♡ A, as opener would think that his partner was looking to him to control the diamond suit.

THE SPLINTER BID

This is simply an alternative way of sending the same message as that transmitted by a fragment bid. This time you bid the singleton suit instead of the suit in which values are held.

OPENER   RESPONDER
1 ♣   1 ♡
4 ◊

Playing splinter bids, 4 ◊ shows the values for a raise to 4 ♡ with a singleton diamond. A bid of 3 ♠ in this sequence would also be a splinter bid.

The Poor Man's Ace

The void suit, when a strong fit in trumps is present, has been called the poor man's ace, and it undoubtedly represents a potent force. Identifying a void during the bidding not only establishes that the partnership has control of this suit but also enables the partner of the void player to appraise his hand more accurately: He knows that any high cards he holds in this suit are likely to be wasted. Conversely, when he has little or nothing in this suit, his hand is likely to play above its face value since his points will be exceptionally productive.

By partnership agreement, a double jump bid that has no natural meaning can be used to show a void suit and a fit with partner. Thus:

(a) | OPENER | RESPONDER |
     |--------|-----------|
     | 1 ♣ | 1 ♠ |
     | 4 ◇ | |

(b) | OPENER | OPPONENT | RESPONDER | OPPONENT |
     |--------|----------|-----------|----------|
     | 1 ♡ | 1 ♠ | 2 ♣ | Pass |
     | 3 ♠ | | | |

In each case opener is showing a void and agreeing to his partner's suit. (Obviously the 4 ◇ in (a) cannot be used if you are playing either splinter or fragment bids.)

The next example illustrates the dramatic revaluation that may arise when a void-showing bid is used.

OPENER	RESPONDER
♠ A K 9 5 4 3	♠ 6
♡ J 9	♡ A 8 3
◇ A Q 8 4 2	◇ K J 9 7 5 3
♣ —	♣ J 8 6

OPENER	RESPONDER
1 ♠	2 ◇
5 ♣ (a)	5 ♡ (b)
7 ◇ (c)	Pass

(a) Opener is worth a raise to 5 ◇ on values. So, for the same money, he may make the void-showing bid of 5 ♣.

(b) Responder started out with a bare minimum but (1) he may add two points because it is clear that there is a 10- or 11-card trump suit, and (2) he has virtually no wasted values in clubs. Responder is willing to bid 6 ◇, but he shows ♡ A in case opener can bid 7 ◇

(c) There will obviously be a play for this contract even if responder has no useful cards other than ♡ A and ◇ K.

Void-showing bids, it will be seen, occupy the same space as fragment bids. Both cannot be used. Since singletons are more common than voids, it would seem that devotees of fragment bids have the better of the bargain.

Trump Solidity

Many slams hinge on the soundness of the trump suit: There may be ample material for twelve tricks, but if there are two losers in the trump suit, it is unreasonable to expect a happy outcome. That, of course, is why the principle of not bidding bad suits in good hands is held in such high regard.

Against that, there are many situations where the auction proceeds more smoothly when a moderate four-card suit may be introduced at some stage. This practice should therefore be subjected to a condition: A weak suit should not be bid when there is any possibility that partner, holding appreciable undisclosed values, may take off into a slam with this suit as trump. For example:

	OPENER	RESPONDER
	1 ♡	2 ♣
	?	

Opener holds:

♠ J 10 4 2   ♡ A K Q 8 3   ◇ A 5   ♣ K 4

To bid 2 ♠ here would be risky. As the responder's hand is unlimited, after this powerful rebid there would be a danger that he might force the bidding to 6 ♠ with an inadequate suit. The rebid, therefore, should be 3 NT. If partner had previously passed, there would be more to be said for 2 ♠; the responder could not then have the values to bid a slam, and the exploratory bid of 2 ♠ might lead to a better contract.

When slam is under consideration, the attraction of a 4-4 trump fit always presents a possible trap for good players, for it is well known that a 4-4 fit is often superior to 5-4 in this type of hand:

♠	A 8 7 3	♠	K 9 4 2
♡	A K Q 8 2	♡	J 10 5 4
◇	4	◇	A 9
♣	K 7 3	♣	A 6 2

With hearts as trumps, declarer must expect to lose a club trick and a spade. With spades as trumps, a club can be discarded on the fifth heart and the twelfth trick made by ruffing a club. A spade slam in fact presents no problems as long as the outstanding spades are 3-2.

The snag is that the search for a 4-4 fit too often results in a trump suit such as A-9-x-x opposite 10-x-x-x. This may be satisfactory at the level of game or part-score, but a slam in such a suit is hard to make. So, when it is clear that your side has excellent values, sufficient for twelve tricks, do not go out of your way to play in a 4-4 trump suit. Instead, concentrate on selecting the most *solid* trump suit, whether this is 5-4, 4-4, 5-3 or 6-2. When you cannot rely on the soundness of any trump suit, play at 6 NT.

The Grand Slam Force

Point count and other aids to valuation may become quite unnecessary when a really big trump fit is present. In a hand like the following it is easy to see that thirteen tricks will roll in as long as there is no loser in the trump suit.

OPENER	RESPONDER
1 ♣	1 ♡
1 ♠	3 ♠
?	

Opener holds:

♠ Q 8 4 3 2   ♡ —   ◇ A 7   ♣ A K Q 10 6 3

Opener is prepared to take his stand at 7 ♠ if partner's spade support includes the A-K, for the remaining features of his hand can hardly matter. Since a Blackwood sequence is not likely to help, the Grand Slam Force has been invented to help discover these vital cards. Here, opener makes a direct jump to 5 NT, an otherwise idle bid. Partner is then required to bid seven of the agreed trump suit, irrespective of his other holdings, if he has two of the three top honors in this suit—the ace, king or queen. Lacking two of these honors, he signs off at six of the agreed suit. Clearly, then, you do not bid 5 NT unless you have one top honor yourself, nor do you bid 5 NT unless you are willing to be in six.

The Grand Slam Force, sometimes known as "Josephine" after Josephine Culbertson, who is credited with its invention because she was the first to write about this ingenious brainchild of Ely's, is popular and gives rise to no ambiguity. It cannot be confused with Blackwood, for you cannot bid a Blackwood 5 NT, asking for kings, without first bidding 4 NT to ask for aces. A 5 NT bid is *never* the Grand Slam Force when there has been a bid of 4 NT.

Excellent though this convention is, the responses are clearly open to improvement, and many variations are employed by regular partnerships. The following simple scheme can be recommended:

        6 ♣ No top honor (A, K or Q)
        6 ◇ One top honor
        6 ♡ Two top honors
        6 ♠ Three top honors

This scheme is useful on many more hands than the original convention.

BARON GRAND SLAM TRY

A different method of probing the trump suit, known as the Baron Grand Slam Try, can be used when "Josephine" is not available, such as when there has been a Blackwood bid of 4 NT. This consists of a bid of six in the suit *below the agreed trump suit*. Partner is asked to bid seven in the agreed trump suit if his trumps are "good," which of course means good in relation to his previous bidding. This convention can be used in a very wide variety of hands. One example will illustrate its flexibility.

OPENER	RESPONDER
♠ K 4	♠ A J 7
♡ A J 6	♡ 8
◇ A K Q 10 7 6	◇ J 5 3
♣ 8 3	♣ A K 10 7 4 2

OPENER	RESPONDER
1 ◇	2 ♣
3 ◇	4 ◇ (a)
4 ♡ (b)	4 NT
5 ♡	6 ♣ (c)
7 ◇ (d)	Pass

(a) After opener's strong rebid, responder's only problem is whether to bid 6 ◇ or 7 ◇ . He is prepared to gamble that there will be no losing clubs, and that if necessary this suit can be established by ruffing. For the moment he bids 4 ◇ , setting the trump suit.

(b) A normal cue bid, showing the ace. This is made below the level of game and does not signify extra values.

(c) After checking the aces, responder uses the Baron Grand Slam Try, saying: "Bid 7 ◇ if your trumps are good."

(d) Opener's bidding has already suggested a strong six-card diamond suit. Accordingly, he would not be justified in bidding the grand slam with anything less than his actual holding or with A-K-x-x-x-x-x.

The Swiss Convention

When the "limit" double raise of partner's suit is in use, showing about 11 or 12 points, it can be difficult to express a stronger hand, about 13-16 points, which would formerly have been shown via a forcing double raise. Suppose that your partner opens 1 ♠ and you hold:

♠ K Q 9 8   ♡ A J 4 2   ◇ 5 3   ♣ K J 4

This hand is much too strong in high cards for a raise to 4 ♠ . It is true you may make a waiting bid of 2 ♣ and jump to 4 ♠ on the next round. But this does not give an ideal description of the hand, for partner may well place you with a biddable club suit.

The Swiss Convention uses the responses 4 ♣ and 4 ◇ over a major-suit opening, which are virtually non-existent in the natural sense, for hands of this kind. In one popular version a response of 4 ♣ shows good controls and a response of 4 ◇ shows exceptional trump support. Many variations of the convention are in use, and some tournament players extend it to the minor suits. Thus over 1 ♣ the responses of 3 ◇ and 3 ♡ are "Swiss," and so on. The usual scheme of responses by the opening hand is that a simple rebid of opener's own suit is a sign-off and all other bids are slam invitations.

The most constructive use of the Swiss Convention occurs when it forms part of an overall plan for all types of responding hands that contain primary support for opener's suit and game-going values. A scheme popular among players who favor limit double raises is this:

A direct raise to game shows very strong trump support with less than 10 high-card points.

A minimum bid in a new suit followed by a jump to game in opener's suit shows at least the equivalent of opening values, with strong trump support and a biddable side suit.

A Swiss bid of 4 ♣ or 4 ◇ also shows opening values and strong support but no biddable side suit.

A normal jump shift, followed by support for opener's suit on the next round, shows at least 16 points including a biddable side suit.

The Losing Trick Count

This is a method of valuation devised in the United States by Dudley Courtenay and revised in Britain by the late Maurice Harrison-Gray, who fashioned from it a very handy way of appraising a hand for play at an agreed trump suit. It is used by many experts, especially in Europe.

When a satisfactory trump fit has been found—at least eight cards in the two hands—each player counts his "losers" as follows:

Count one loser for each missing high honor (ace, king or queen) in each suit, ignoring the fourth and subsequent cards in any suit. Thus K-x-x-x-x counts as two losers; the ace and queen are missing, but the fourth and fifth cards are not counted.

Do not count more losers than you have cards in the suit. Thus a void or singleton ace counts as no losers; a singleton other than the ace is one loser; a small doubleton is two losers; A-x and K-x are also one loser, but Q-x is two losers.

The number of losers in your hand will indicate how high you should bid in the agreed trump suit.

APPLYING THE LOSING TRICK COUNT

A sound minimum opening is assumed to contain seven losers. A responder who raises his partner's opening may add the losers in his own hand to the opener's expected seven losers. The total is deducted from 18—the key number in LTC—and the resulting figure indicates how high you should bid.

OPENER	RESPONDER
♠ A 10 7 4 2	♠ Q 8 6 3
♡ 8	♡ K J 4 2
◇ K Q 6 3	◇ 8 2
♣ K 8 2	♣ A 10 3

The opening bid is 1 ♠ and the responder, with sound support for this suit, applies the Losing Trick Count. He has two losers in each suit, eight in all. Adding this figure to the seven expected in his partner's hand, and deducting the total from 18, he is worth a raise to 3 ♠.

Opener, too, may apply LTC when rebidding. In the above example he has only six losers: two in spades, one in hearts, one in diamonds and two in clubs. Since his partner has shown eight losers, he deducts the total from 18 and raises to four, a reasonable contract.

Opener may also use LTC when raising his partner's suit. In this case he assumes that the responder holds nine losers for a bid at the one-level, eight for a response at the 2-level. Suppose the bidding goes:

OPENER   RESPONDER
1 ♣   1 ♠
?

Opener holds:

(1) ♠ A J 6 3   ♡ A Q 4   ◇ J 3   ♣ Q 10 9 3
(2) ♠ Q J 8 4   ♡ A 7   ◇ 9 2   ♣ K Q J 5 3
(3) ♠ Q 10 8 7   ♡ 2   ◇ A Q 10   ♣ A K J 6 2

In (1) opener has seven losers: two in spades, one in hearts, two in diamonds and two in clubs. This is consistent with a minimum opening, so he raises only to 2 ♠. Opener may arrive at the same answer by adding his seven losers to partner's expected nine losers: the total deducted from 18 indicates a contract of two. Of course, if the responder has in fact fewer than nine losers, he will take it from there.

In (2) opener has six losers: two in spades, one in hearts, two in diamonds and one in clubs. This is one less than a normal opening, so he raises not to 2 ♠ but to 3 ♠. It will be seen that LTC attaches considerable weight to distributional features: here, opener has fewer points in high cards than in the previous example, yet his hand is stronger.

In (3) there are only five losers. These, added to partner's nine and deducted from 18, indicate a contract of four. Opener may therefore raise straight to game, make a fragment bid of 4 ◇ or make a splinter bid of 4 ♡.

LTC WHEN REBIDDING

LTC can be used as a yardstick by a player who has to decide whether his hand is worth a strong rebid. A jump rebid in opener's own suit should not usually be made with more than five losers.

OPENER	RESPONDER
♠ K 2	♠ A 10 8 4 3
♡ K Q 9 8 4 3	♡ A 7 2
♢ A 8 7	♢ Q 10 6 2
♣ A 6	♣ 10

OPENER	RESPONDER
1 ♡	1 ♠
3 ♡ (a)	6 ♡ (b)
Pass	

(a) With two losers in diamonds and only one loser in each other suit, opener is worth a jump rebid.

(b) With three-card support opposite a known six-card suit, responder can apply LTC to see how high to raise. He has seven losers which, added to partner's five and deducted from 18, indicate a slam in hearts. The use of LTC at slam level is, of course, normally subject to a checkup on controls.

In the same way, LTC requirements are laid down for other strong bids and rebids. A reverse bid by the opener usually indicates a five-loser hand, or six with a high point count. A jump rebid by responder in his own suit shows six losers.

THE "JUDGMENT" FACTOR

From this brief description the reader will realize that the use of LTC calls for a good deal of common sense. It is obvious, for example, that A-x-x is a far better two-loser holding than Q-x-x. This is allowed for by "balancing" aces against queens, and by counting a queen as three losers when it is not supported by the king or jack and there is no ace against which it can be balanced. Your partner opens 1 ♠ and you hold:

(1) ♠ A 8 7 2   ♡ Q 9 6 4   ♢ A 6   ♣ Q 8 2
(2) ♠ Q J 7 4   ♡ K Q 4 2   ♢ Q 8 6   ♣ 10 4

With (1) you have seven losers in support of spades, as the two queens may be balanced against the two aces. Hand (2) has eight losers, for there is no ace against which to balance ◇ Q-x-x. The other two queens are not counted as losers because they are supported. In the same way the combination A-J-10 is usually worth at least as much as A-Q-x and is counted as one loser.

DEDUCTING LOSERS FOR FAVORABLE FEATURES

Either partner may deduct a loser for certain favorable features. When the responder has five-card support for his partner's suit he may deduct a loser for "trump control." When the opener knows of at least ten trumps in the combined hands, he too may deduct a loser for "super trump control." Either player may deduct a loser when he has an above-average holding of aces, or when he has a key feature that is well placed. Partner opens 1 ♠ and you hold:

♠ K Q 4 3   ♡ A 10 8 6 2   ◇ A 9 7   ♣ 10

You have two aces that are not balanced against queens, so you should deduct a loser and call this a five-loser hand, which means you are in slam range. You do not bid a slam direct, of course, but you do intend to reach 6 ♠ opposite no more than a sound minimum opening if you can establish that the hands fit reasonably well and that there are not two inevitable losers.

5

Scientific Sequences

♠ ♡ ◇ ♣

"Reverse" Rebids by Opener—The Jump Rebid by Opener—Opener's Simple Rebid in a New Suit—The Responder's Rebids

The term "scientific bidding" is applied loosely—and by some disparagingly—to sequences in which the partnership hands are developed in a series of "approach" bids rather than with one or two broadly descriptive bids. The Scientists represent one of the two extreme wings of bidding theory, the other consisting of the "Bashers." The reader will no doubt have encountered numerous examples of both species. He may wonder, however, whether an entire chapter on scientific sequences is really needed, as the virtues of simple and direct bidding have been so warmly commended.

Simple and direct bidding, alas, although it is highly desirable, must sometimes be abandoned in the interest of greater precision. It is right to bid straight to the best contract whenever possible, but there are some hands that need detailed exploration, and you should be willing, when necessary, to undertake this task. Indeed, when close investigation is really needed, your motto should be, "We pry harder." Some of these exploratory sequences have been hinted at in the previous chapters, and it is now proposed to fill in the gaps.

"Reverse" Rebids by Opener

First, a definition: A "reverse" by opener is a strong rebid, at least 17 points, and its characteristic feature is that, although not a jump bid, it pushes the bidding high.

(1)	OPENER	RESPONDER	(2)	OPENER	RESPONDER
	1 ♣	1 ♠		1 ♠	2 ♡
	2 ◇			3 ♣	

It will be seen that the opener has bid his suits in reverse of the normal sequence; hence the term. The responder cannot return to opener's first suit below the level of three-odd; that is why opener needs a strong hand for these sequences. It is also a firm requirement that opener should have at least five cards in his first suit.

There are two types of reverse bid: a low reverse as in (1) where the bid is made at the 2-level; and a high reverse where the second suit is shown at the 3-level as in (2). There is no necessary difference in the strength shown, but there can be quite a difference in the forcing quality of the sequences that follow.

THE LOW REVERSE

When responder has bid at the one-level, a reverse bid by opener is not forcing. He may have no more than 17 points and the responder may have no more than 6. When the responder has bid at the 2-level, however, there will usually be at least 27 points in the combined hands. A reverse bid by opener is then forcing; indeed, it is unrealistic to suppose that the bidding will stop short of game unless the hands turn out to be a rather bad misfit.

(1)	OPENER	RESPONDER	(2)	OPENER	RESPONDER
	1 ◇	1 ♠		1 ♡	2 ♣
	2 ♡			2 ♠	

The first is a non-forcing sequence, the second is forcing. Even in such sequences as (1), however, there are not very many hands with which the responder will elect to pass.

It is necessary to have a clear idea as to which bids by the responder at this point will be weak and which will be strong. Suppose that in the first sequence the responder holds:

(1) ♠ A J 8 3   ♡ 7 6 2   ◇ 9 4   ♣ Q 10 5 4
(2) ♠ K Q 10 8 6 3   ♡ 7 4   ◇ J 2   ♣ 9 7 5
(3) ♠ A K 7 2   ♡ 10 6 4   ◇ 8 7 4   ♣ 9 3 2

With (1) the responder's next bid should be 2 NT, which shows a guard in the unbid suit but a minimum hand. With only two or three more points he would jump to 3 NT. With (2) responder bids 2 ♠, showing a rebiddable suit but very little else. The third hand is a common type where the correct call is not a pass but 3 ◇. Remember that when the opener reverses, his first suit will be at least five cards, and he will be justifiably exasperated if you leave him in a shaky 4-3 fit when he could have played in a much safer 5-3 combination, albeit at one level higher.

The bids described in the last paragraph are all weak and non-forcing, any other bid being constructive. It follows from the third example that the responder must at all costs avoid the simple return to opener's first suit—simple preference, as it is called—if his hand enables him to visualize game opposite opener's strong bidding. For example:

OPENER	RESPONDER
1 ♣	1 ♠
2 ♡	?

Responder holds:

(1) ♠ K Q J 8 3   ♡ 7 3   ◇ 9 2   ♣ K 7 6 4
(2) ♠ A 10 7 4 3   ♡ Q 10 5 2   ◇ 9 6   ♣ Q 3
(3) ♠ A Q 3 2   ♡ 10 4 3   ◇ K J 6   ♣ 9 7 5

With none of these hands should you be willing to stop below game after partner's strong bidding. With (1) you jump to 4 ♣, as 3 ♣ would be a weak bid. Do not be put off by the fact that a minor-suit game is a long way to go: You have 12 points in support

of clubs, and this is your partner's party. He may be able to bid
4 ♠, which in this sequence would be a natural bid, not a cue bid.

With (2) a raise to 4 ♡ stands out. Partner has shown at least
17 points and you have more than enough support for game, including a key card, ♣ Q. With (3) you have a handy rebid of 3 NT.

When the responder's first bid was made at the 2-level, showing a minimum of 10 points, it may be anticipated that there will be
at least 27 points in the two hands. It will be realistic now to treat the
situation as forcing to the 4-level. In other words, the bidding may
stop below game only if the partnership settles in a minor suit, and
then only when it is clear that there are not 29 points in the two
hands.

OPENER	RESPONDER
♠ J 3 2	♠ 9 5
♡ A J 10 4	♡ K Q
◇ K Q J 10 3	◇ 7 5 4
♣ A	♣ K J 9 8 6 4

OPENER	RESPONDER
1 ◇	2 ♣
2 ♡	3 ◇ (a)
4 ◇ (b)	Pass (c)

(a) This is a more disciplined bid than 3 ♣ because there is
sure to be at least a 5-3 fit in diamonds.

(b) Since opener knows that this bid may be passed, it follows
that he would have to jump to 5 ◇ with a stronger hand holding no
future in any other suit.

(c) Responder has a minimum hand and it is clear that his
values are not working outstandingly well.

When the responder has bid at the 2-level, any rebid below
game over opener's reverse is forcing. Thus responder does not
have to go straight to game every time he has good values. When

there is the possibility of alternative contracts, or a slam, he can afford to proceed slowly.

OPENER   RESPONDER
1 ♡   2 ♣
2 ♠   ?

Responder holds:

(1) ♠ A 9 8 6   ♡ 4   ◇ A 8 3   ♣ K J 8 5 4
(2) ♠ Q 10 7   ♡ 8   ◇ A Q 3   ♣ K 10 8 4 3 2
(3) ♠ J 9 2   ♡ Q 8   ◇ J 10 3   ♣ A Q 10 9 3

Opposite opener's strong bidding, (1) and (2) are powerhouse hands and responder is keenly interested in the possibility of slam. However, the bidding can be developed slowly, as opener will not pass any simple bid. With (1) you bid just 3 ♠ for the moment, to set the suit and test partner further. If opener now bids 4 ♠, this will be a sign that he has little or nothing in reserve, but you will still be worth a cue bid of 5 ◇. However, if partner were to bid 4 ♣ over 3 ♠, you could expect your club suit to be worth several tricks at a spade contract. Nothing would now keep you out of 6 ♠ except the misfortune of being afflicted with an aceless partner—most unlikely.

With (2) the slam prospects depend more heavily on whether opener holds secondary club support. The best temporary move is not 3 ♣ but 2 NT. If partner bids 3 ♣, you are in business. If he simply raises to 3 NT, you had best give up, for now the hand is unlikely to be a good enough fit.

Hand (3) is of more modest proportions. You feel confident of making game, but the best denomination is in doubt. The correct rebid is 3 ♡, on the principle that a 5-2 fit (it may be 6-2, of course) is normally preferable to a 4-3 fit. If opener bids 3 NT over 3 ♡ you intend to pass.

THE HIGH REVERSE

When the responder has bid at the 2-level, a 3-level bid by opener in a third suit can be used to develop even the most powerful hands. As in the case of a low reverse, there will be at least 27 points in the two hands and the sequence will be forcing to at least four of a minor suit. Opener will have a minimum of five cards in his first suit, but the length of his second suit is less clearly defined. This second suit will not necessarily be shorter than the first; the opening hand could be something like this:

♠ A K J 8 5   ♡ Q 2   ◇ K Q J 7 3   ♣ 6

With this hand you would open with 1 ♠ and over partner's response of 2 ♡ you would rebid 3 ◇, showing reversing values. If partner instead responds 2 ♣, you of course rebid 2 ◇. The difference is that partner does not know at this stage that you have such a strong hand.

However, the high reverse is a common and almost indispensable maneuver with a *three*-card suit also.

OPENER	RESPONDER
1 ♠	2 ♡
?	

Opener holds:

(1) ♠ A Q 9 4 2   ♡ Q 7   ◇ J 10 3   ♣ A K J
(2) ♠ A J 8 5 3 2   ♡ K Q 2   ◇ A 9 2   ♣ 7
(3) ♠ K 9 8 7 6 4   ♡ A 4   ◇ A 2   ♣ A J 9

The most satisfactory way of developing each of these hands is by bidding a three-card minor on the second round. With (1) 3 ♣ is the only sound move: Opener hopes that his partner can rebid no-trump, but he intends to raise a rebid of 3 ♡ to game and convert a club raise to 4 ♡. Hand (2), with its excellent controls and strong support for responder's known five-card heart suit, is well worth a direct raise to 4 ♡, but first opener should bid 3 ◊. If responder now shows positive support for spades, opener's hand will become even stronger. In any case he intends to continue by supporting hearts, giving a picture of the singleton club, which may be a key feature for slam. With (3) it is advisable to avoid committing the hand in any one strain. A rebid of 3 ♣ will ensure reaching the best contract, which may be either 4 ♡, 4 ♠ or 3 NT.

After a high reverse by opener, much depends on the exercise of good judgment by the responder. Here is an example of how the bidding may develop.

OPENER	RESPONDER
♠ A Q	♠ 9 6 3
♡ Q 10 8 4 2	♡ K J 7
◊ A J	◊ K 10 9 7 5
♣ K Q J 4	♣ A 7

OPENER	RESPONDER
1 ♡	2 ◊
3 ♣	4 ♡
4 ♠	5 ♣
5 ◊	5 ♡
6 ♡	Pass

There are two key bids in this auction. First, there is opener's rebid of 3 ♣, which is more exploratory than 3 NT. Then there is responder's jump to 4 ♡ on the second round. Without this assurance that responder's heart support is excellent, opener would be very loath to push on to 6 ♡ with such a sketchy suit even though his hand is in many ways well-suited to slam.

Quiz on Reverse Sequences by Opener

Your partner opens 1 ◇ and rebids 2 ♡ over your response of 1 ♠. What would you bid now with each of the following?

(1) ♠ A Q 10 9 7 2   ♡ K 3   ◇ 7 2   ♣ J 9 3
(2) ♠ K 9 7 5 4   ♡ 10 7 2   ◇ 8 3   ♣ A J 10
(3) ♠ A K 7 5 2   ♡ Q 7   ◇ K J 8 4   ♣ 10 4
(4) ♠ K 8 5 3 2   ♡ J 7 3   ◇ 2   ♣ J 7 5 4
(5) ♠ K Q 9 3   ♡ 7 5 2   ◇ Q 4   ♣ K J 10 4

Your partner opens 1 ♡ and rebids 2 ♠ over your response of 2 ♣. What would you bid now with each of the following?

(6) ♠ J 3   ♡ J 7 2   ◇ K 4 2   ♣ A Q 10 4 2
(7) ♠ K 7 3   ♡ 10 2   ◇ A Q 4   ♣ K Q 4 3 2
(8) ♠ Q 7   ♡ A Q 9   ◇ 7 5 3   ♣ K 10 9 6 3
(9) ♠ J 3   ♡ 7   ◇ 7 4 2   ♣ A Q J 9 7 4 2
(10) ♠ K Q 7 4   ♡ 10 2   ◇ 8 5   ♣ A Q 9 8 3

Solutions

1. 3 ♠. A simple rebid of 2 ♠ would not be forcing after the initial one-level response. A bid of 3 ♠ shows that you have a good six-card suit and the values for game opposite a reverse.
2. 2 NT. This is natural and non-forcing. With two or three more points, a jump to 3 NT would be in order.
3. 4 ◇. This hand is far too strong for a simple preference bid of 3 ◇, which could be passed by partner. The jump to 4 ◇ establishes a forcing situation.
4. Pass. Partner's reverse bid is not forcing after a one-level

response. If you are ever going to pass a reverse, this can hardly be an inappropriate occasion.

5. 3 NT. A bid of 2 NT would not be forcing in this sequence. You should jump to game, for it is clear that the combined hands contain game-going values.

6. 3 ♡. This is better than bidding notrump, as partner may be very unbalanced. Because the situation is forcing, you do not need to jump to 4 ♡. Thus the hand may still be played in 3 NT if partner, too, has a diamond guard.

7. 2 NT. There must be a good chance of slam after opener's strong rebid, but the best denomination is uncertain. You should therefore afford opener the chance to describe his hand further. This hand is rather too strong for 3 NT, which would be a suitable bid with two or three points fewer.

8. 4 ♡. Because 3 ♡ would be forcing, this jump preference bid shows that you have excellent trump support for partner's known five-card suit.

9. 3 ♣. Partner may not pass this bid, but it will be possible to stop at 4 ♣ should it turn out that the hands do not fit.

10. 4 ♠. Again this "unnecessary" jump to game can be used to show especially strong trump support, and it may encourage opener to push on to a slam.

The Jump Rebid by Opener

This strength-showing rebid has many characteristics of a reverse bid by opener. It tends to be in the 17-19 point range; it is unconditionally forcing when responder has bid at the 2-level; and it is non-forcing, though strongly encouraging, when responder has bid at the one-level. It differs from a reverse in that it proclaims, of course, a one-suited hand, based usually on a strong six-card suit.

♠ K 4   ♡ A J 10 9 3 2   ◊ A K 4   ♣ 9 6

With this hand you would open 1 ♡ and rebid 3 ♡ over any simple takeout by partner. A jump rebid in a minor suit tends to suggest a slightly stronger suit than this, and usually a final contract of 3 NT is very much in mind.

Because a jump rebid by opener is such a highly descriptive bid, the responder's next action will usually be clear-cut. The important point to note is that any rebid by responder below game level is forcing. Suppose you are the responder in this sequence:

OPENER	RESPONDER
1 ♡	2 ♣
3 ♡	?

You hold:

(1) ♠ A 10 8 3   ♡ 7   ◇ 10 4 2   ♣ K Q J 5 4
(2) ♠ 7 3   ♡ Q 8 6   ◇ A Q 10 3   ♣ K J 7 2
(3) ♠ 8 7 4 3   ♡ 10   ◇ A 9 5   ♣ A K 6 5 3

With (1) you want to be in 3 NT if partner has a diamond guard, and you therefore bid 3 ♠. It is very unlikely that partner will ever raise this call, for with a four-card spade suit he would probably have reversed into 2 ♠ on the second round. Accordingly, this type of rebid by responder is also a common and useful maneuver with a three-card suit.

With (2) you have a small problem, though a pleasant one. A raise to 4 ♡ would not do justice to your hand, for partner might well pass with a hand that could produce a slam. Therefore the best move is 4 ◇. On the next round, over any minimum bid by partner, you intend to bid 5 ♡, inviting partner to bid slam if he is strong and can control the spade suit.

Hand (3) presents a problem that can occur in almost any phase of the bidding process: One player has shown a good hand with a strong suit, and his partner has useful values but no support for this suit. In this situation the responding hand should not fear to raise with remarkably little trump support, provided that his values in the side suits consist of quick tricks that are certain to be of use to partner. Here the responder may bid 4 ♡ with reasonable confidence. The bid to avoid is 3 NT.

Opener's Simple Rebid in a New Suit

There are some powerful hands that do not slot neatly into any of the strong rebids that are available to the opening hand. Opener may then have to keep the ball rolling by means of a simple rebid in a new suit. The disadvantage of such a call is that it is not forcing and makes little progress toward a clearer definition of opener's strength. It may be based on anything from a sub-minimum opening to one that narrowly fails to qualify for a jump-shift rebid. The following is the type of strong hand that has to be treated in this way.

♠ K 7 2   ♡ A Q 10 5 3   ◇ 4   ♣ A K 8 3

Suppose you open 1 ♡ and partner responds 1 ♠. Promising though your hand is, you should not raise to 3 ♠ with three-card support, nor have you the values for 3 ♣. You must therefore be content with 2 ♣. The responder will not often pass, but if he does it's a case of "C'est la guerre." If, as is much more likely, responder does find another bid, you will be able to complete an accurate picture of your hand, as the sequence may continue like this:

OPENER	RESPONDER
1 ♡	1 ♠
2 ♣	2 ♡
2 ♠	

This may well be classed as a scientific sequence, but it is a case where science is a good cause, for the 2 ♠ bid is highly descriptive. It suggests three-card spade support, a singleton diamond and a distinctly strong hand; with a medium or minimum hand the opener would have bid 2 ♠ on the previous round.

Opener may also make a simple change of suit on a strong hand when he is anxious to explore the possibility of a major-suit fit.

♠ K Q 7 3   ♡ Q 10   ◇ A 4   ♣ A Q J 5 3

You open 1 ♣ and partner responds 1 ♡. You have the values for a jump to 2 NT, but there is nothing in the auction so far to suggest that your partner does not hold a four-card spade suit. A rebid of 1 ♠ is therefore preferable. If this does not unearth a fit, you can still bid notrump on the next round; alternatively, opener may make a still more effective bid on the next round by bidding the fourth suit. Suppose that, with the hand above, the auction has proceeded:

OPENER	RESPONDER
1 ♣	1 ♡
1 ♠	2 ♣
?	

Opener does not really want to play in notrump unless partner has a diamond guard. Also, if this guard consists of, say, Q-x-x, it may be advantageous for responder to become declarer. Furthermore, opener is very willing to play at a heart contract rather than at notrump if responder has a six-card suit. On all grounds, therefore, the scientific bid of 2 ◇, the fourth suit, is best. Obviously, partner will not assume, in this sequence, that this is a genuine suit.

The Responder's Rebids

Quite often, when it is time for the responder to make his second bid, he is in a position to bring matters to a conclusion. When a trump suit has been agreed, the techniques described in Chapter 4 will show how high to go. When the hand belongs in notrump, a simple count of points will frequently supply the answer. There are, however, some powerhouse hands that require further investigation, and it is proposed now to describe the forcing bids that still remain at responder's disposal.

RESPONDER BIDS A THIRD SUIT

Because new-suit bids by responder are forcing, a certain minimum level of strength is needed The following sequences are presented in approximate order of strength.

```
        OPENER    RESPONDER
        1 ♣       1 ♠
        2 ♣       2 ♡
```

Opener's rebid shows a minimum or near-minimum one-suited hand that is unlikely to contain more than 15 points. Thus there is little purpose in the introduction of a third suit by the responder except when he still has hopes of game. Either he must be very close to opening values or he must have a pronounced two-suiter. Here is an example of each type:

(1) ♠ K Q 7 4 2   ♡ A 10 9 3   ◇ 8 2   ♣ Q 6
(2) ♠ Q J 8 6 4 2   ♡ K Q 9 8 7   ◇ 4   ♣ 7

Hand (1) represents about the minimum strength for a constructive bid of 2 ♡; with any weaker hand the responder does better in the long haul to pass 2 ♣. Hand (2) is an example of the distributional type; again, with any weaker hand the responder is advised to pass 2 ♣. Opener may be expected to go down several tricks at this contract, but the golden rule with misfit hands is to stop bidding before you are doubled.

A *reverse* rebid by responder, as in the next sequence, suggests a stronger hand:

```
        OPENER    RESPONDER
        1 ◇       1 ♡
        2 ◇       2 ♠
```

Like all reverse sequences, this one conveys that responder has at least five cards in his first suit. Opener is expected to take forceful action if his hand is reasonable in the light of the previous bidding.

♠ K 2   ♡ J 10 4   ◊ A Q 9 6 4 3   ♣ K 5

With this hand the opener, in the sequence above, should jump to 4 ♡, as a bid of 3 ♡ could be passed.

In the next sequence the responder's rebid is stronger still, as the bidding cannot in practice stop below the level of 3 NT or four of a suit.

OPENER	RESPONDER
1 ♡	2 ◊
2 ♡	3 ♣

This bid of a new lower-ranking suit at the 3-level is one of the most versatile moves available to the player who has a powerful responding hand with which, for one reason or another, he did not make an immediate jump shift. It is based presumptively on a holding that can withstand being led through at notrump, such as K-10-x. (By "presumptively" I mean that the opener is entitled to act on this presumption; responder may perhaps not have this holding, but in that case it's his party—he will be able to handle the situation.) This bid of a third suit at the 3-level also warrants that partner will not be left hanging if his next bid is short of game, and it thus brings stability to the auction. Some example hands:

OPENER	RESPONDER
♠ 9 4	♠ A Q 8 3 2
♡ A K J 8 3	♡ 10 5
◊ K Q 4	◊ J 7 3
♣ 7 6 2	♣ A K 8

OPENER	RESPONDER
1 ♡	1 ♠
2 ♡	3 ♣
3 NT	Pass

This is a straightforward example of the usefulness of this bid. Responder bids 3 ♣, hoping his partner can go to 3 NT with a diamond guard. Failing this, the responder, with a wealth of quick tricks, is willing to let his partner play at 4 ♡. As it happens, opener is able to oblige.

The next case presents a sterner test of good bidding.

OPENER	RESPONDER
♠ A Q 10 7 4 3	♠ 9 2
♡ Q 4	♡ A K 8 7 3
◇ K 8 4	◇ A J 10
♣ 10 4	♣ J 5 2

OPENER	RESPONDER
1 ♠	2 ♡
2 ♠	3 ◇
3 ♡ (a)	3 ♠ (b)
4 ♠ (c)	Pass

(a) A bid of 3 ♠ would work satisfactorily on this occasion, but this would be a poor choice as partner might well have a single-ton spade and a six-card heart suit.

(b) This is the type of trustful bid that helps to build a good partnership. Responder's bid of 2 ♡ over 1 ♠ showed a five-card suit, and it is to be presumed that opener would have raised straight-away if he held 5-3 in spades and hearts. Responder does not know that his partner has six spades, but he does know that (1) the values for game are present, (2) there is evidently no game in notrump and (3) if 4 ♡ is a better spot than 4 ♠, opener will assuredly return to that suit.

(c) The best contract.

There is one situation where a bid in a new suit by responder is not forcing. This occurs when opener rebids 1 NT, as here:

	OPENER	RESPONDER
	1 ♣	1 ♡
	1 NT	?

Now a new-suit bid of 2 ◇, as well as the bids of 2 ♣ and 2 ♡, will not be forcing because opener has limited his hand. But a "reverse" bid of 2 ♠ counts as forcing, and most players treat any jump bid as forcing.

RESPONDER BIDS THE FOURTH SUIT

It sometimes happens that the first three bids of the auction are all in different suits and yet the best denomination is still unclear. The responder may be faced with what appears to be an impossible task in a situation like this:

	OPENER	RESPONDER
	1 ♡	1 ♠
	2 ♣	?

Responder holds:

♠ A 10 8 4 2   ♡ J 3   ◇ J 7 3   ♣ A K 4

With opening values in both hands the responder does not wish to stop below game, but the best denomination may be 3 NT, 4 ♡ or 4 ♠, depending on the nature of the opener's hand. What is responder to bid at this point? He cannot bid notrump missing a diamond guard, nor is his hand suitable for 3 ♡ or 3 ♠.

To cope with this type of "unbiddable" hand, the practice has grown-up of bidding the fourth suit as a forcing maneuver when no sound natural bid is available. In this example, therefore, responder bids 2 ◇. Now opener's next bid will indicate where the hand should be played.

The use of the fourth suit in this sense is thoroughly recommended (provided, of course, that your partner sees eye to eye with you). When the partnership has already bid three suits, it is seldom that the responder will wish to put forward the fourth suit as a trump-suit possibility. Used in this sense, a bid of the fourth suit at the 3-level proclaims opening values. At the 2-level it may be made on slightly less—11 or 12 points—because the bidding may still stop at 2 NT.

Once having adopted the principle of using the fourth suit as an artificial forcing maneuver, it can be very good style to extend the use of this bid to hands where a natural bid is available but is less than ideal.

OPENER	RESPONDER
1 ◇	1 ♡
2 ♣	?

Responder holds:

♠ A 4 2   ♡ K Q J 5 3   ◇ 8 4   ♣ K J 6

The responder has the values for a jump to 3 NT, and this is the bid he would have to make if he were not playing "fourth suit forcing." However, 2 ♠ is a better bid. If opener does not bid notrump over 2 ♠ but shows belated support for hearts, 4 ♡ will surely prove to be the soundest contract. Moreover, if opener does bid notrump, having a holding such as Q-x-x or K-J-x in spades, the contract will be played by the safer hand. If, over 2 ♠, opener can only rebid 3 ◇, responder can still go to 3 NT himself.

Opener's first obligation when his partner has bid the fourth suit is to convert to notrump if he has a guard in this suit, remembering to jump to game when he has the necessary values.

OPENER	RESPONDER
1 ♡	2 ♣
2 ◇	2 ♠
3 NT	

The responder is expected to have at least 11 points in this sequence, so opener may jump to game with a healthy-looking 15 points. Here, if opener bids only 2 NT, responder may pass.

When opener cannot bid notrump for lack of a guard in the fourth suit, he simply makes the most descriptive bid available. Rather than rebid one of his own suits, he should show delayed support for the responder's first suit if possible. Moreover, he should afford jump support whenever his hand is better than it might be. On occasion this may provide the means of reaching a slam contract that would otherwise be elusive.

OPENER	RESPONDER
♠ A K 9 4	♠ 6 2
♡ J 7 2	♡ A K Q 9 3
◇ 3	◇ J 5 2
♣ A Q 10 5 4	♣ K 7 2

OPENER	RESPONDER
1 ♣	1 ♡
1 ♠	2 ◇
3 ♡	

Here the responder has a problem on the second round, and the best solution is a bid of the fourth suit. Opener should appreciate that his partner's failure to bid notrump may be significant: There is probably little wastage in diamonds and, as responder has shown near-opening values, it is right for opener to jump to 3 ♡. Now it is his partner's turn to exercise his imagination: After this fluent start it should be possible to reach the sound contract of 6 ♡ by means of a cue-bidding sequence (as described in Chapter 7).

The use of the fourth suit as a forcing cypher does not prevent a genuine fit in this suit from being brought to light. The bidding goes:

OPENER	RESPONDER
1 ♠	2 ♣
2 ◇	2 ♡
?	

Opener holds:

♠ A Q 4 3 2   ♡ Q 9 7 2   ◇ A Q 10 3   ♣ —

Responder has not promised a biddable heart suit, but all the same opener should raise to 3 ♡, showing four-card length. This bid is forcing, and opener's sequence, of course, denotes extreme shortage in clubs.

THE JUMP REBID IN RESPONDER'S SUIT

This rebid, too, is forcing. It shows opening values and a sound six-card suit.

OPENER	RESPONDER
1 ♡	1 ♠
2 ♡ (2 ♣, 2 ◇)	3 ♠

Responder holds:

♠ A K J 9 5 2   ♡ 10 4   ◇ 7 3   ♣ K 8 2

This represents about the minimum hand for such a sequence.

Responder may bid the same way with an appreciably stronger hand.

A special inference arises when the responder rebids his suit one range higher, at the level of game.

OPENER	RESPONDER
1 ♡	1 ♠
2 ◇	4 ♠

This tends to suggest that responder is encouraged by opener's second bid. He may have a strong hand with a very poor holding in opener's first suit, which is why he did not respond with a jump shift.

Quiz on Responder's Rebids

Your partner opens 1 ♡ and rebids 2 ♣ over your response of 1 ♠. What is your bid on the following hands?

(1) ♠ K J 8 6 2   ♡ 10 4   ◇ A 9 7 3   ♣ Q 5
(2) ♠ K Q 7 6 3   ♡ Q 4   ◇ A 5 2   ♣ K 10 3
(3) ♠ A K 7 4 3   ♡ 9 5   ◇ A Q J   ♣ Q 10 3
(4) ♠ K 9 8 7 3   ♡ Q 4   ◇ A 5 2   ♣ 7 3 2
(5) ♠ Q J 10 9 4 2   ♡ 8 3   ◇ A 4   ♣ A 9 8

Solutions

1. 2 NT. This hand is not quite strong enough for a fourth-suit bid of 2 ◇, which in any case is not needed when a satisfactory natural bid is available.

2. 2 ◇. You have game-going values, but the best contract is

in doubt and a scientific bid of the fourth suit will surely help. If partner is able to bid notrump, that will settle matters; if he rebids in either of the major suits, game in that major is likely to be safer than in notrump.

3. 3 NT. This honest descriptive bid is preferred to a forcing but uninformative bid of 2 ◇. If partner has a strong balanced hand he may be able to raise to 6 NT, whereas if you were to bid 2 ◇ you might easily get tied up in knots.

4. 2 ♡. Here you are not strong enough for a bid of 2 ◇, which would suggest at least 11 points. Thus 2 ♡ is the solution, for opener is very likely to have a five-card suit and the hand may be expected to play better in hearts than in a 4-3 club fit.

5. 3 ♠. This hand represents a sound minimum for this forcing rebid, showing opening values and a sturdy six-card suit. It would be wrong to bid 2 ◇, the fourth suit, when an adequate descriptive bid is available.

6

Powerhouse Sequences in Response to Notrump

♠ ♡ ◇ ♣

The Jump Response to 1 NT—The Stayman Convention—The Balanced Powerhouse Opening—The Flint Convention—The Texas Convention—Jacoby Transfers

Because the standard openings of 1 NT and 2 NT both show strong hands, 16-18 and 21-22 points respectively, these bids will often act as a springboard for reaching game or slam when the responder also has fair values. Still more is this so when an artificial 2 ♣ opening is followed by a rebid of 2 NT showing 23-24 points or 3 NT showing 25-26.

All opening bids of that kind are *good* bids and should be employed whenever possible. They have much in common. The strength of opener's hand is shown within narrow limits, as is his distribution, which can only be 4-3-3-3, 4-4-3-2 or 5-3-3-2. Responder's job, when he has a promising hand, is to press home this advantage by commonsense methods and with the aid of two or three useful conventions which will shortly be described.

In responding to any bid in notrump, the golden rule is that when responder can see the best contract, as is very often the case, he should straightaway bid it. Suppose that your partner opens with a standard 1 NT and you have these hands:

(1) ♠ 9 8   ♡ 10 7   ◇ A K J 9 5 3   ♣ 8 6 3

(2) ♠ J 10 8 5 3 2   ♡ K 7   ◇ 6   ♣ A 8 4 3
(3) ♠ 2   ♡ Q 9 8 6 4 3   ◇ 10 7 5   ♣ J 8 7

With (1) any response but 3 NT is pointless, yet players have sometimes been known to call 3 ◇. There are two ways in which retribution may set in. First, the opener, if his hand seems suitable for a diamond contract, may be trusting enough to bid 4 ◇: there is now no assurance of making any final contract. Secondly, if opener rebids 3 NT, the defenders will have a better idea what to lead. I am not suggesting that the opponents might have led a diamond if this suit had not been mentioned; rather, now that they know a long minor suit is in the offing, they are better able to judge whether to conduct an active or passive defense.

Incidentally, if you are in any doubt as to whether this hand has potential for slam, you can easily verify that it has not. Assume that your partner has a maximum hand with support for diamonds. Now you may add points for shortness in your hand as well as length—but the total is still only 30 points.

With (2) the same principle applies: 4 ♠ must be the right contract, so you should bid it over 1 NT. Hand (3) illustrates the important principle that when the combined hands cannot total 26 points, responder aims to drop the bidding in the safest partial. Here you bid 2 ♡, a sign-off.

There are of course many hands where despite the highly descriptive nature of the 1 NT opening the responder cannot immediately select the final contract. We now consider how these hands may be developed, assuming a standard 1 NT of 16-18 points. (The same principles apply if the range is 15-17 points, 13-15 or even 12-14. You simply adjust the number of points required by the responder for each bid.)

The Jump Response to 1 NT

A bid of 3 ♣, 3 ◇, 3 ♡ or 3 ♠ in response to 1 NT is forcing. Its primary meaning is to offer opener a choice between game in this suit and game in notrump. The minimum strength is 10 points, ensuring a combined count of at least 26. A five-card or longer suit is an essential requirement; hands containing no suit of more than four cards may be introduced by means of the Stayman Convention.

Over 1 NT a response of 3 ♥ or 3 ♠ is much more common than the responses of 3 ♣ or 3 ◊, which are seldom made unless there is at least some interest in slam. However, one does not bid 3 ♥ or 3 ♠ on *every* hand that contains game-going strength and a five-card major suit. These bids are made only when there is reason to think that game in a 5-3 trump fit will be safer than 3 NT. Your partner opens 1 NT and you hold these hands:

(1) ♠ A   ♥ Q J 9 8 3   ◊ 10 9 4 3   ♣ Q J 5
(2) ♠ K Q J 8 3   ♥ 8 5 4   ◊ 10 2   ♣ A 5 2

It is usually right to seek a suitable trump contract on any hand containing a singleton. With (1), therefore, you would bid 3 ♥, especially since a spade opening lead could leave the dummy hand short of entries in a contract of 3 NT. With hand (2) it is different. Nine tricks at notrump, with the opening lead going up to your partner's hand, may be easier than ten tricks in spades, with the initial lead coming through opener's holdings in hearts or diamonds. Moreover, at a notrump contract your card of entry, ♣ A, will not be readily dislodged. With this hand, therefore, you are not so attracted to the 5-3 trump suit; you would be more inclined to raise to 3 NT. Alternatively, as a 5-4 fit is very favorable indeed, you might first bid 2 ♣ (Stayman) to see whether opener has four spades.

There is also scope for anticipation on the part of the 1 NT bidder. When he proposes to raise responder's suit, he may be able to indicate, without going beyond game, that his hand is suitable for a slam. Thus:

OPENER	RESPONDER
1 NT	3 ♠
?	

Opener holds:

♠ K Q 8 3   ♡ A 2   ◇ K J 8 4   ♣ A 10 7

Because opener's hand is so extremely promising in support of spades, he should not simply raise to 4 ♠ but should bid 4 ♣. This says, "I have good support for spades, I have ♣ A and my hand is suitable for a slam if that is what you have in mind." (This is the technique of the Advance Cue Bid, described in Chapter 7.)

Opener may sometimes be able to cooperate in a slam venture even when he has only three-card, or even two-card, support for his partner's suit. Suppose that you open 1 NT and your partner responds 3 ♠. You hold:

♠ K 4   ♡ A Q 9   ◇ A 10 9   ♣ A 10 7 3 2

For the moment you must bid 3 NT, since you have only two spades. Suppose that partner continues with 4 ♠. Now it is clear that he holds at least a six-card suit and that he was interested in slam (otherwise he would have made an immediate bid of 4 ♠). With such excellent controls your hand is very suitable, so you should go straight to 6 ♠.

The Stayman Convention

This has proved one of the most durable of all bidding conventions, for most systems incorporate a 2 ♣ inquiry for major suits in response to an opening bid of 1 NT. A vast number of variations have been proposed over the years, but even the best of these are only marginally more efficient than the original. It is proposed, therefore, to dwell only upon what is generally regarded as "Standard Stayman."

Over an opening bid of 1 NT, a response of 2 ♣ asks the opener to bid a four-card major suit; without one, the opener replies

with a conventional 2 ◇. The bidding then proceeds along commonsense lines. Suppose your partner opens 1 NT and you have this
hand:

♠ J 10 9 3   ♡ A Q 5 2   ◇ 8 2   ♣ A 10 3

You have ample strength for a raise to 3 NT, of course. But if
opener has four hearts or four spades, it is likely that the trump
contract will be safer. Therefore you bid 2 ♣. If partner bids 2 ♡
or 2 ♠, you bid game; a raise to three would not be forcing. If
partner responds negatively with 2 ◇, you bid 3 NT.

A Stayman bid of 2 ♣ does not necessarily signify game-going
values. It may be used also when the responder can do no more than
invite game. For example:

♠ Q 10 8 4   ♡ 7   ◇ K J 8 4   ♣ Q 10 9 3

If you were not playing the Stayman Convention, you would
raise your partner's 1 NT opening to 2 NT. As it is, you bid 2 ♣
first. Over 2 ◇ you intend to bid 2 NT, showing a hand of this
strength. If you receive a favorable response of 2 ♠, however, your
hand will improve and will become worth a raise to 4 ♠. This can
be verified by the use of point count: Your hand is worth 10 points
in support of spades, and your partner's minimum is 16.

The advantage of playing in a suitable 4-4 major-suit fit is in
fact greater at slam level than at game level. (At game level you
have to be able to make *two* more tricks in the major suit before you
are better off than in a notrump contract.) The Stayman Convention
is therefore valuable with a hand like the following:

♠ K J 10 2   ♡ K 4   ◇ A 10 8 7   ♣ A 8 3

You could raise partner's 1 NT opening to 4 NT, asking him to
pass with a minimum and bid 6 NT with a maximum. It is better,
however, to bid 2 ♣. If partner responds 2 ♠, you are prepared to

undertake 6 ♠ whether or not he has a maximum. If he bids 2 ◊ you can still bid 4 NT, which will not be Blackwood since no suit has been agreed upon.

When the opener has length in both major suits, it does not matter much which suit he bids first. It is presumed that the 2 ♣ bidder has four cards in at least one major suit,* so the opener can take the pressure off his partner in a sequence like the following:

OPENER	RESPONDER
1 NT	2 ♣
2 ♠	2 NT
?	

Opener holds:

♠ A 9 8 6   ♡ K 10 9 3   ◊ A Q   ♣ K J 5

The correct bid now is 4 ♡! Opener may assume that his partner has a four-card heart suit and was intending to raise a response of 2 ♡ to at least 3 ♡. With this very suitable collection, opener should not risk falling short of game.

FORCING REBIDS BY THE 2 ♣ BIDDER

There is much scope among regular partners for the development of forcing sequences after a Stayman bid of 2 ♣ and the conventional response. Many partnerships treat a rebid of 3 ♣ or 3 ◊ by responder as forcing to game.

(1)		(2)	
OPENER	RESPONDER	OPENER	RESPONDER
1 NT	2 ♣	1 NT	2 ♣
2 ♡ (2 ◊, 2 ♠)	3 ♣	2 ◊ (2 ♡, 2 ♠)	3 ◊

*Innumerable variations on the Stayman Convention are in use among regular partners. Some players do not guarantee a four-card major when they bid 2 ♣.

In each case the responder is showing a five-card minor suit and is inviting opener to say whether his hand is suitable for slam in this suit. If opener now bids 3 NT, this is a sign-off. Any other call shows at least a tentative willingness to play at a slam contract, with the responder's minor suit as trumps.

Since a 4-4 trump fit will often produce an extra trick, it must be sound, at the level of slam, to play in a 4-4 minor suit when one is available. Some regular partnerships use a second-round jump to 4 ♣ or 4 ◇ , after a Stayman sequence, to investigate this possibility. This is sometimes called the Sharples Convention.

OPENER	RESPONDER
1 NT	2 ♣
2 ◇ (2 ♡, 2 ♠)	4 ♣ (or 4 ◇)

The responder is showing specifically a four-card minor suit, and he is inviting opener to cooperate in a slam if he too has four cards in this suit. The sign-off is 4 NT. The convention is very effective on hands of 4-4-3-2 pattern that would present no more than borderline play for slam at notrump. To illustrate:

OPENER	RESPONDER
♠ K 4 2	♠ A 8 5
♡ A Q	♡ K 7 4 2
◇ Q 10 7 5	◇ K J 9 3
♣ A Q 8 3	♣ K 2

OPENER	RESPONDER
1 NT	2 ♣
2 ◇	4 ◇ (a)
4 ♡ (b)	4 ♠ (c)
5 ♣ (d)	6 ◇ (e)
Pass	

(a) The Sharples Convention, showing a four-card diamond

suit. Opposite a 16-18 point notrump, a minimum of about 14 points in high cards is needed for this bid.

(b) This cue bid shows the ace of hearts and guarantees that at least four diamonds are held.

(c) Normal cue bid.

(d) With a slightly less promising hand, opener would bid 4 NT, which could be passed, instead of offering this second cue bid.

(e) Opener has no four-card major, so is likely to have at least three-card length in clubs. Responder can therefore expect his own shortage in this suit to produce at least one extra trick.

Quiz on Responding to 1 NT

Your partner opens 1 NT, showing 16-18 points. What is your response with the following hands?

(1) ♠ K 4 2   ♡ K 10 8 5 3   ◊ A 7 4 2   ♣ 8

(2) ♠ Q J 7 5   ♡ K 8 4 2   ◊ 7 5   ♣ 10 6 3

(3) ♠ Q 6 4 3   ♡ A Q 9   ◊ K J 8   ♣ K 10 7

(4) ♠ A 4 2   ♡ 10 7 3   ◊ K Q J 7 5   ♣ J 8

(5) ♠ A 8 6 3   ♡ 7 5   ◊ 10 3   ♣ K Q 7 4 2

Solutions

1. 3 ♡. This hand contains the values for a raise to 3 NT, but with a singleton it is advisable to consider a trump contract. You do not bid 2 ♣ with this type of hand, for you need only to find your partner with three hearts, not four.

2. Pass. Perhaps it would be pleasant to bid 2 ♣ and alight in a 4-4 major-suit fit at the 2-level. But if your partner were to respond negatively with 2 ◊, you would have no safe rest-

ing place. A bid of 2 ♡ or 2 ♠ over 2 ◇ would announce a five-card suit and would risk playing in a 4-2 fit; a rebid of 2 NT would invite partner to bid game.

3. 4 NT. This direct raise invites partner to bid 6 NT or pass. With such a completely balanced hand there is no guarantee that a 4-4 spade fit would produce an extra trick, or would not result in a losing slam contract in spades opposite K-x-x-x.

4. 3 NT. This is the most likely game contract, and therefore you should bid it. A bid of 3 ◇ would suggest at least some interest in slam and might put entirely wrong ideas into your partner's tiny little mind.

5. 2 ♣. This is a very suitable hand for the Stayman Convention. If no 4-4 spade fit comes to light, you intend to raise to 3 NT on the next round.

The Balanced Powerhouse Opening

It was noted in Chapter 2 that the modern—and strongly recommended—scheme for dealing with balanced powerhouse openings is as follows:

21 or 22 points— (exceptionally, a "good" 20)	Open with 2 NT.
23 or 24 points—	Open with 2 ♣ and rebid notrump at the minimum level.
25 or 26 points—	Open with 2 ♣ and jump to 3 NT over a 2-level response. (After a positive 3-level response—3 ♣ or 3 ◇—you would not stop short of slam.)

This prospectus applies when the artificial game-forcing bid of 2 ♣ is employed. For players who use Forcing 2-bids, the scheme is this:

20 or 21 points—	Open with one of a suit and rebid 3 NT.
22 to 24 points—	Open with 2 NT.
25 or 26 points—	Open with 3 NT.

Note that the structure of the subsequent bidding by both hands is largely unaffected by the scheme that is in use. In each case the vital guidelines are the same, suitable adjustments being made to the number of points required. Thus the *type* of hand with which the responder would elect to explore for a suit contract, or try for slam, is no different, whether his partner's 2 NT opening shows 21-22 points or 22-24. Having made this observation, I will not mention it again and will assume that the 2 ♣ opening is in use.

RESPONDING TO 2 NT

By bidding 2 NT the opener proclaims to his partner that he has 21 or 22 points; exceptionally, a 20-point hand with several tens or a nice-looking five-card suit. Endowed with such a very satisfactory start in life, it is certainly worthwhile to develop the bidding with more than ordinary care. Yet this is an area in which many disasters occur, even in a high-standard game. These are usually due to the responder's failure to show his hand accurately by means of one of the three basic responses: the immediate bid of game, the exploratory response of 3 ♡ or 3 ♠, and the conventional 3 ♣ response.

The Immediate Bid of Game

A bid of 4 ♡ or 4 ♠ is natural, based on a six-card or longer suit. *It is also conclusive*. Responder is simply not interested in anything better, and opener is obliged to pass. (However, you should make sure partner is of the same mind as you about this bid. Some players use this response as a mild slam try.) Over your partner's 2 NT opening you would jump happily to 4 ♡ with a hand no stronger in high cards than this:

♠ 7 3   ♡ Q 9 8 4 3 2   ◇ 10 4   ♣ Q J 3

The Response of 3 ♡ or 3 ♠

It follows from the preceding that if the responder has a long major suit and a hand that offers any chance of slam, he must take things more slowly. Suppose this is your hand:

♠ K 10 9 7 5 2   ♡ A 10 3   ◇ 9 7 2   ♣ 5

Opposite an opening bid of 2 NT, this hand may produce a slam if partner is strong and has good controls. You should first bid 3 ♠. Opener may be able to make an immediate cue bid, indicating spade support and a hand suitable for slam. However, if opener rebids 3 NT, you continue with 4 ♠. Now opener may reappraise his hand: The sequence 2 NT-3 ♠-3 NT-4 ♠ must logically be constructive, for otherwise you would have jumped to 4 ♠ immediately.

A more frequent use of the response of 3 ♡ or 3 ♠, however, is to cover the large range of responding hands, usually of 5-3-3-2 distribution, where you have to choose between game in a major suit and game in notrump, one of the most critical of all decisions.

Generally, the responder to 2 NT should not fail to show a five-card major suit, even a very weak one. Moreover, the opener should raise this suit whenever he has three-card support, even though he has the other three suits well held. Thus there is a stronger tendency to play in a 5-3 trump suit after a 2 NT opening than after a 1 NT opening. One reason for this is that the responding hand will often be short of entries and accordingly the five-card suit may be useless unless it is the trump suit. Another reason, also concerned with entries, is seen in this common type of deal:

OPENER	RESPONDER
♠ K J 2	♠ A 8 7 4 3
♡ A K 5	♡ J 6
◇ K Q 10 3	◇ 8 4 2
♣ K Q 10	♣ 7 5 3

OPENER	RESPONDER
2 NT	3 ♠
4 ♠	Pass

4 ♠ is not exactly a brilliant contract, but declarer can at least enter his hand with ♠ A and try the trump finesse, subsequently reentering with a heart ruff in an attempt to develop the minor suits. At 3 NT the shortage of entries to the weak hand will oblige declarer to duck a round of spades, foregoing the chance of the finesse. The likelihood is that he may be able to lead only once from dummy during the whole hand.

When the responder has a stronger hand, a response of 3 ♡ or 3 ♠ may be the first move in a slam investigation, especially when the opener can cooperate by showing a suitable hand. This example shows both players taking advantage of slender indications.

OPENER	RESPONDER
♠ A J 7 4	♠ K Q 10 8 3
♡ A Q 9	♡ 10 8 2
◇ K 10	◇ A 7 2
♣ A K 8 3	♣ 7 4

OPENER	RESPONDER
2 NT	3 ♠
4 ♣ (a)	4 ◇ (b)
4 ♡	4 ♠ (c)
6 ♠ (d)	Pass

(a) Opener does not simply make a lazy raise to 4 ♠ but cue-bids ♣ A.

(b) A bid of 4 ♠ now would conclude the auction. As it is, responder has barely enough to suggest a slam: He has ten points, including distribution, and may now add a point for the club shortage. The combined count, therefore, could just be sufficient.

(c) Despite opener's second cue bid, responder signs off. He has shown the full strength of his hand.

(d) Opener's hand could not be more suitable for a slam so he disregards the sign-off.

In effect, once the responder shows mild slam interest by cue-bidding ◇ A, opener intends to reach at least a small slam. His cue-bidding maneuvers are necessary, however, as responder may have a grand slam in mind.

The Conventional 3 ♣ Response

The standard meaning of 3 ♣ over 2 NT is a normal Stayman inquiry: Opener bids 3 ◇ with no major suit, and if the responder continues with 3 ♡ or 3 ♠, this shows a five-card suit. This rebid is useful when responder has 5-4 in the major suits.

♠ J 8 7 4 3   ♡ A 9 4 2   ◇ 7 3   ♣ Q 6

If over an opening bid of 2 NT the responder were to bid 3 ♠, he might miss a superior fit in hearts. He therefore bids 3 ♣, continuing over 3 ◇ with 3 ♠.

A variation employed by some experts is known as the Baron 3 ♣ bid. This invites the 2 NT opener to show four-card suits "up the line." The bidding continues until a fit is found or 3 NT is reached. Thus:

OPENER	RESPONDER
2 NT	3 ♣ (Baron)
3 ◇ (a)	3 ♡ (b)
3 NT (c)	Pass

(a) Four-card diamond suit.

(b) Four-card heart suit.

(c) No four-card spade suit.

The advantage of the Baron 3 ♣ bid is that it will always uncover a 4-4 fit in diamonds and sometimes in clubs. (Opener shows a balanced hand containing four clubs by bidding 3 NT over 3 ♣, thus denying any other four-card suit.) But it is sometimes less effective than the Stayman Convention when responder is 5-4 in the major suits.

RESPONDING AFTER 2 ♣-2 ◊-2 NT

The machinery for showing a balanced powerhouse by opening at 2 ♣ and rebidding in notrump has been discussed in Chapter 2. As for the responses, they are similar to those over a direct 2 NT opening.

OPENER	RESPONDER
2 ♣	2 ◊
2 NT	?

Now that the opener has shown 23 or 24 points, the responder proceeds as if his partner has *opened* 2 NT, showing this strength. In other words, a direct bid of 4 ♡ or 4 ♠ is a sign-off, 3 ♡ and 3 ♠ are exploratory, and 3 ♣ is conventional.

Quiz on Responding to 2 NT

Your partner opens at 2 NT. What do you bid on the following hands?

(1) ♠ 8 6 3   ♡ Q 8 4 3   ◊ J 7 4 2   ♣ 5 3
(2) ♠ Q J 4 3   ♡ J 10 3   ◊ K 8 5   ♣ Q 4 3
(3) ♠ 5 3   ♡ Q J 8 6 4 2   ◊ Q 6 2   ♣ 10 8

(4) ♠ 10 7 2 ♡ K 3 ◇ A 8 7 5 ♣ K J 6 2
(5) ♠ K 10 7 5 4 3 ♡ 7 2 ◇ A 8 3 ♣ J 4

Solutions

1. Pass. Opener's maximum is 22 points. A balanced hand with 3 points is not enough for a raise to game, and the chance of finding opener with a four-card heart suit by bidding 3 ♣ is not good enough to warrant jeopardizing a plus score.
2. 3 NT. With 9 points opposite a maximum of 22 there can be no slam in the hand, and no point in searching for a possible 4-4 spade fit. If you were 4-4-4-1 or 4-4-3-2 you might contemplate an exploratory sequence and a subsequent slam try with these values.
3. 4 ♡ This is a sign-off that opener is expected to pass irrespective of the nature of his hand.
4. 4 NT. This is a natural raise of notrump. Partner is expected to bid 6 NT with 22 points and to pass with less.
5. 3 ♠. A slam may well be there if partner has good controls and a suitable hand. If he rebids 3 NT, you intend to continue with 4 ♠, showing a hand of this type.

The Flint Convention

No mention has been made of the response of 3 ◇ over 2 NT. The standard practice is to use this as a natural bid, showing at least five diamonds and interest in a possible slam. But among tournament players 3 ◇ is widely used as an artificial bid to cover a quite different type of hand.

Suppose that your partner opens at 2 NT and you hold either of these two hands:

(1) ♠ 6 2 ♡ 10 8 7 6 4 3 ◇ 6 ♣ 10 8 3 2
(2) ♠ J 8 7 4 3 2 ♡ 6 ◇ 9 5 2 ♣ 10 8 3

To incur a minus score with a powerhouse hand is always regrettable and here it is painfully clear that the only makable contract is likely to be three in the long major suit. Such a contract is unattainable in standard methods because partner will bid again over 3 ♡ or 3 ♠. Playing "Flint," however, you bid 3 ♢ with each of the two hands and your partner is compelled to bid 3 ♡! With the first hand you now pass, and with (2) you bid 3 ♠, which opener passes.

The original convention was as simple as that. Theorists soon realized, however, that the idea could be developed still further, and it is now possible to handle the situation where the 2 NT bidder has such suitable cards that he is willing to reach game opposite a six-card major suit in an otherwise worthless hand. For example, suppose you hold this opening hand:

OPENER	RESPONDER
♠ A 6	♠ 9 4 3
♡ A J 9 4	♡ 10 8 7 6 5 2
♢ A K 8 2	♢ 6 4
♣ A J 5	♣ 8 4

OPENER	RESPONDER
2 NT	3 ♢ (Flint)
?	

Dull would he be of soul who was unwilling to take a stab at 4 ♡ with this rockcrusher opposite a responding hand with six hearts. However, playing the basic version of the Flint Convention, there is a difficulty: opener cannot jump straight to 4 ♡ because partner's suit may be spades. And if opener simply bids 3 ♡, responder will pass.

Playing "Extended Flint," the opener, when he has a wealth of top cards and strength in one of the major suits, follows this ingenious procedure:

With good support for hearts he bids 3 ♠! If responder's suit is hearts, he converts to 4 ♡. If it is spades, he passes.

With good support for spades opener bids 3 ♡, and if responder converts to 3 ♠, the opener raises to 4 ♠.

With good support for both major suits opener bids 3 NT over 3 ♡, leaving partner to name the suit.

In the preceding hand, therefore, opener would bid not 3 ♡ on the second round but 3 ♠, and responder would correct to 4 ♡. When the opener has no great strength in either spades or hearts, he simply bids 3 ♡, as in the basic version.

Playing either basic Flint or Extended Flint, it is still possible to show a hand with which you would make a natural response of 3 ♢. For example, suppose your partner opens 2 NT and you hold:

♠ 10 9 6   ♡ Q 8 2   ◇ K 10 8 4 3   ♣ A 2

You bid 3 ♢ and continue with 3 NT over partner's next bid. This sequence shows that you do not have a "Flint-type" hand at all: You have a diamond suit and are interested in slam.

The Texas Convention

Suppose that your partner opens with 1 NT or 2 NT and you have a long major suit, worthy of a direct bid of game. It may be that your prospects would be still more favorable if, instead of playing the hand yourself, you could make partner the declarer with this suit as trump. The Texas Convention is designed for that purpose.

♠ Q 10 9 7 6 4   ♡ 2   ◇ 8 5 3   ♣ A Q 3

If partner opens 1 NT and you have this hand, you respond not with 4 ♠ but with the conventional bid of 4 ♡. Now partner is required to convert to 4 ♠, which you pass. The advantage is that your partner's hand is concealed, which may make life more difficult for the defenders. Also, you are more likely to gain a trick from the opening lead with the notrump hand as declarer than with your own hand as declarer.

In the same way, if your partner opens at notrump and you have a string of hearts, you bid a conventional 4 ◇ and your partner converts to 4 ♡. In each case you are following the "transfer" principle of bidding the suit next in rank below your true suit.

There is, however, a human difficulty with this convention: Players who since time immemorial have been treating the sequence 1 NT-4 ♡ as simply a good honest bid have been known to pass the Texas bid of 4 ♡—with rather poor results. A version known as South African Texas is therefore preferred by many players. According to this variation, instead of bidding the suit below your true suit as a transfer request, you bid 4 ♣ over 1 NT to ask opener to bid 4 ♡, and you bid 4 ◇ to ask him to bid 4 ♠. As the jump to 4 ♣ or 4 ◇ hardly exists in a natural sense, the danger of a memory lapse is avoided.

Both versions of the convention can be used in the same way over an opening bid of 2 NT. The transfer principle has also been extended by some players to *opening* bids at the 4-level. Thus an opening bid of 4 ♣ asks partner to bid 4 ♡, and an opening 4 ◇ asks for a transfer to 4 ♠. It is now possible to treat opening bids of 4 ♡ and 4 ♠ as normal weak preemptive bids while the transfer openings of 4 ♣ or 4 ◇ are slightly stronger.

Jacoby Transfers

In studying the Flint Convention the reader may have been struck by the multiplicity of bids that can be set in motion by the artificial response of 3 ◇ over 2 NT. This is in fact a characteristic of all "transfers": They lead to greatly increased productivity, so to speak.

Jacoby Transfers exploit this by applying the transfer principle to the simple responses to 1 NT. Instead of bidding 2 ♡ to show a heart suit, you bid 2 ◇; this requires opener to bid 2 ♡. In the same way a response of 2 ♡ over 1 NT shows spades and requires opener to bid 2 ♠.

The advantage is very great. First, you may employ the transfer as a means of settling in a contract of 2 ♡ or 2 ♠ as at present, but with the strong hand now concealed. You may also use it with the sort of hand in which you intend to make a try for game. In this case the effect of the transfer is that responder can show his hand with remarkable accuracy at a safe level.

For example, suppose your partner opens 1 NT and you have this hand:

♠ K 10 8 7 4   ♡ J 8 6   ◇ Q J 2   ♣ 7 3

You respond with 2 ♡, showing a spade suit. Your partner duly bids 2 ♠ and now you continue with 2 NT. This shows that you have the values for a normal raise to 2 NT over 1 NT, about 7 points. But meanwhile, of course, you have also managed to show the five-card spade suit.

In the next example responder has a hand that must be played in the major suit, but he can leave opener to decide how far to go.

OPENER	RESPONDER
1 NT	2 ◇ (Transfer)
2 ♡	3 ♡

Responder holds:

♠ 6   ♡ Q 10 8 7 4 3   ◇ A J 4   ♣ 7 3 2

This sequence suggests a six-card suit. Opener may either pass or bid 4 ♡.

Another striking example of the efficiency of the transfer bid is seen here:

OPENER	RESPONDER
1 NT	2 ♡ (Transfer)
2 ♠	3 ♣

This sequence can be used to show a five-card suit and a secondary club suit. Opener is expected to bid game if he has a maximum hand or a good fit. A typical hand for responder would be:

♠ A 9 8 6 5   ♡ 2   ◇ J 10 4   ♣ K 7 6 3

In tournament play many regular partners employ an agreed scheme of defense against the use of transfer bids by their opponents. Suppose the bidding has gone:

SOUTH	WEST	NORTH	EAST
1 NT	Pass	2 ◇ (Transfer)	?

Now fourth hand may proceed as follows:

(a) A double of the artificial bid shows strength in this suit.

(b) A bid of the opponent's genuine suit is equivalent to a takeout double of that suit. Thus 2 ♡ in the above example would show a spade suit and support for the minors.

(c) A bid of 2 NT shows both minor suits.

(d) With a strong balanced hand, fourth hand may pass to await developments.

Returning to the opening side, it is best to arrange that transfers are abandoned when there is immediate interference. For example:

SOUTH	WEST	NORTH	EAST
1 NT	2 ◇	?	

A bid by North in either major suit will be natural.

7

Slam Tries, Cue bids
and Controls

♠ ♡ ◇ ♣

Ace-showing Cue Bids—Second-Round Controls—The Grand Slam Try—The Advance Cue Bid—The Blackwood Convention—The Gerber Convention

To reach an unmakable slam contract hurts more than missing a makable slam, even though logic tells us that both mishaps are equally calamitous. Accordingly, in this sector of bidding there is a well-established tendency toward caution. When there is a choice between a safe game and a problematical slam, the principle that commends itself to most players is that a sparrow in the kitchen is worth a canary on the roof.

However, it follows that it is in precisely this sector that players can most improve their results. It is true that slam hands occur in only about one deal in ten, but they greatly affect your net plus or minus result. Many experts consider one of the main reasons for Italy's astonishing record in the world team championship is their superior slam bidding.

There are two vital steps in successful slam bidding. First you must assess whether your side has the power to make twelve tricks. Secondly you make sure that the opponents, who have the opening lead, cannot take the first two tricks. The first of these is usually the more exacting task.

To establish the sequence of thought, let us take a clear example.

```
        OPENER    RESPONDER
         1 ♠        4 ♠
         ?
```

Opener holds:

♠ K 10 8 4 3   ♡ A 6   ◇ A K 10   ♣ K J 7

Here the responder is expected to hold about 13 points, mainly distributional. Opener started out with 19 points and may add at least one now that his five-card suit has been strongly supported. Alternately, he can value his hand at six losers and deduct one for trump control. Either way, a contract of 6 ♠ is indicated. Opener therefore bids 4 NT. But even if partner shows two aces, opener does not dream of bidding 7 ♠, for he still expects to have the material for no more than twelve tricks. The determining factor is *strength*. The number of aces is important, but usually in a negative sense.

Quite often you cannot safely bid a slam unless you can establish that partner is maximum. This is not much of a problem when you intend to play notrump. If partner opens 1 NT, for example, and you have a balanced 16 count, you can raise to 4 NT, which is non-conventional. This bid of one more than game invites partner to bid 6 NT if he has a maximum. At a trump contract the principle of bidding one more than game to invite a slam would be most unhealthy, by reason of the higher level. A different way of inviting a slam has therefore been devised—the cue bid.

Ace-Showing Cue Bids

A cue bid is a bid in a new suit *when a trump suit has been agreed and the bidding has reached such a level that the partnership is by this time committed to game.* A cue bid shows control of the suit, usually the ace or void, and invites partner's cooperation in reaching a possible slam.

(1)	OPENER	RESPONDER	(2)	OPENER	RESPONDER
	1 ♡	3 ♡		1 ♣	1 ♠
	4 ♣			3 ♠	4 ◇

In each case the last bid must logically be a slam effort—the partnership cannot in any case stop below game, and there would be no point at all in attempting to find a better trump suit. In each case the cue-bidder is saying: "I have the ace (or void) of this suit. A slam is at least a possibility. Are you interested, and can you show a control?" The weakest response the cue-bidder's partner can make is to return to the agreed trump suit at the minimum level.

The advantages of cue bids are considerable. The Blackwood Convention may help you to stay out of slam when the only drawback is that you have too few aces, but it still compels you to play at the 5-level, which may be uncomfortably high. To be able to weigh the chances of slam without going beyond the level of game is far more satisfactory, and frequently the use of cue bids enables this to be done. That is why it is such a great advantage to agree on a trump suit at the lowest possible level, permitting cue-bidding to begin.

Cue bids also have the merit of showing *which* ace is held and, frequently, whether extra values are present. Once the cue-bidding process begins, it may continue with an exchange of several bids. Although a cue bid usually shows first-round control—the ace or a void—it is possible, when these primary controls are present in sufficient number, to show kings and singletons.

This is the sort of hand with which the responder would bid 4 ◇ in the second sequence above, repeated here:

OPENER	RESPONDER
1 ♣	1 ♠
3 ♠	4 ◇

♠ A J 8 4 3   ♡ 7 6 2   ◇ A J 4   ♣ K 10

After his partner's 3 ♠ bid the responder can count on 33 points if opener has 18 points, the middle of his range. So far, this is nothing much to get excited about, but responder's hand includes an invaluable card in opener's first suit. This means that slam is now a probability rather than a possibility. To bid 4 NT, however, would not be very bright, for if opener showed one ace it would not be clear whether there were two quick losers in hearts.

The recommended move therefore is 4 ♢, showing the ace and saying: "If you have the right features, or extra values, a slam may be there. Can you cooperate?" If opener now bids 4 ♡, this will suggest first-round control of hearts and responder may bid 6 ♠ with some confidence. On the other hand, if opener bids 4 ♠ over 4 ♢, indicating no first-round heart control, responder may pause for reappraisal. With even a smidgen less than he has, he would pass. With the actual hand he is worth a bid of 5 ♣, which in this sequence would suggest the king. Now opener knows that he is expected to show signs of life if he has the ♣ A and so much as second-round control in hearts—the king or a singleton. If opener were to bid 5 ♠ over 5 ♣, responder would of course give up.

Here is a situation where it would be wrong to cue-bid:

OPENER	RESPONDER
1 ♢	1 ♠
3 ♠	?

Responder holds:

♠ K Q 10 9   ♡ 10 3   ♢ 8 7 4   ♣ A Q 6 3

It is clear that responder has more than enough for a bid of 4 ♠. It does not follow, however, that he should indicate these extra values by cue-bidding the ace of clubs. Opener has indicated 17-19 points, and responder can revalue his hand at 12 points. Because 31 points will not normally produce twelve tricks, and because there are no redeeming features, the responder should simply bid 4 ♠. The important principle in this example is that a cue bid does not merely show control and extra values: *It indicates that in the cue-bidder's view a slam is at least a possibility.*

CUE BID FOLLOWED BY SIGN-OFF

Suppose that a player makes the first cue bid and then subsides despite an encouraging response from his partner. There is nothing illogical in this; it simply means that this player had barely enough to issue a slam invitation in the first place, and that his partner will have to take all further action if a slam is to be reached.

	OPENER	RESPONDER
	1 ◇	1 ♠
	3 ♣	?

Responder holds:

♠ K J 9 8 3   ♡ 10 4 3   ◇ Q 4   ♣ A Q 3

If forced to take a position at this point, responder would be wise to admit that slam is unlikely: The combined values cannot exceed 33 points, and the value of the queen of diamonds is problematical, depending on just how good partner's suit is. However, there is nothing against bidding 4 ♣. If opener's next move is either 4 ♡ or 4 ◇, responder continues with 4 ♠, making clear his limitations. The 4 ♣ cue bid may be the only encouragement opener needs if his hand happens to be as suitable as this:

♠ A Q 7 2   ♡ 8   ◇ A K J 6 3   ♣ J 7 2

When uncertain whether your hand is worth a cue bid, the *rank* of the suit of this cue bid may be the deciding factor. In the last example the responder was able to make a tentative slam try because his partner, in turn, could reply with a cue bid below game level. Suppose that the bidding goes the same way and this is the responder's hand:

OPENER	RESPONDER
1 ◇	1 ♠
3 ♠	?

♠ K J 9 8 3   ♡ A Q 3   ◇ Q 4   ♣ 10 4 3

Responder has the same values, but his ace is in hearts instead of clubs. It is now inadvisable to bid 4 ♡ with these limited values, for the opener cannot express even the mildest interest without going beyond game level.

It is the same when you are *responding* to a cue bid. Suppose that you are the opener in this sequence:

OPENER	RESPONDER
1 ♣	1 ♡
3 ♡	4 ♣
?	

A bid of 4 ♡ would of course be a sign-off. A bid of 4 ◇ would show control but would not in itself show much in the way of extra strength, for it would not raise the bidding level. However, if you were to bid 4 ♠, taking the bidding beyond the level of game, the message would be: "I am delighted to cooperate. I have the ace of spades and my general values are tiptop."

Cue-bidding is essentially a commonsense process. In this example the player who has to make the key decision is the opener.

OPENER	RESPONDER
♠ A Q J 4 3	♠ K 9 6 2
♡ 4	♡ J 8 2
◇ K 6 2	◇ A 9 7 4
♣ A Q J 7	♣ K 2

OPENER	RESPONDER
1 ♠	3 ♠ (a)
4 ♣ (b)	4 ◇ (c)
4 ♡ (d)	5 ♣ (e)
6 ♠ (f)	Pass

(a) Limit bid.

(b) Now that his suit has been strongly supported, opener may revalue his hand to 21 points, allowing an extra point for "trump control." Playing limit raises, responder's maximum is 12. It is often right to avoid any form of slam try when there cannot be more than 33 points in the combined hands, but here the cue bid is justified by the good controls and the excellent secondary suit.

(c) Responder in fact is maximum and intends now to launch a second slam try even if opener signs off at 4 ♠.

(d) The diamond cue bid has improved opener's hand, so he makes a further slam try. Since opener can already see that there are not two quick losers anywhere in the hand, it is safe to cue-bid this second-round control. Responder may think this shows ♡ A, if he does not have this card himself, but his next move will be nonetheless illuminating.

(e) Responder might well have decided to make this call even if opener had signed off with 4 ♠ over 4 ◇.

(f) It is time for opener to take a position. If partner's 5 ♣ bid is based on the king, slam is likely to be cold. If it is based on a singleton club, this will not be so good, but there will still be a chance of twelve tricks. You should not wait for better odds than this before bidding a slam.

SEQUENCE OF CUE BIDS

When there is a choice of cue bids it is usually right to show the lower-ranking control first. Good sense will suggest some exceptions, however. For example:

```
        OPENER    RESPONDER
        1 ♣       1 ♡
        3 ♡       3 ♠
          ?
```

Opener holds:

♠ 9 2   ♡ K J 6 3   ◇ A 4   ♣ A K 9 8 3

Opener has very sound values and can afford to cooperate in partner's slam effort. Which ace should he show? In general you should tell partner something new rather than something he already knows. In view of the 1 ♣ opening, the responder will assume, if forced into a corner, that there are not two quick losers in this suit. Opener should therefore bid 4 ◇, for otherwise his partner may be unable to proceed due to lack of a control in this suit.

CUE-BIDDING PLUS BLACKWOOD

Good bidding is essentially a two-way street, both partners playing a part in deciding the level of the contract. The player who starts a cue-bidding sequence does not initiate a master-and-slave relationship, as he does with Blackwood. However, either player may bid 4 NT after a cue-bidding sequence has begun. Thus:

```
        OPENER    RESPONDER
        1 ♠       2 ♣
        4 ♣       4 ◇
        4 ♡       4 NT
```

Opener holds:

♠ K Q 10 5 3   ♡ A 6   ◇ J 4   ♣ A Q 9 4

Both 4 ◊ and 4 ♡ are cue bids, with clubs agreed as trumps. Now 4 NT is ordinary Blackwood, perhaps with the intention of continuing with 5 NT to ask for kings. In replying to 4 NT opener still counts any aces he has already shown. Here, with ♡ A and ♣ A, he bids 5 ♡.

Second-Round Controls

As we have seen, cue-bidding is not limited to aces and voids; it is sometimes no less vital to show a king or a singleton. A second-round control can be shown without ambiguity when first-round control of this suit has already been affirmed by either player. There are also occasions when a player may show second-round control with his very first cue bid.

OPENER	RESPONDER
2 ♣	2 ♠
3 ♠	?

Responder holds:

♠ A J 9 5 2   ♡ Q J 7   ◊ K   ♣ J 10 8 2

Clearly 4 ◊ is an attractive move: No doubt opener can tell, or find out, that the responder does not have two aces. In theory 4 ◊ can show a void, but in this kind of sequence a player with a giant hand should assume that his partner is doing the best he can with modest values.

It may even be good tactics to cue-bid a second-round control in preference to a first-round control when this will keep the bidding lower. For example:

	RESPONDER	OPENER
	Pass	1 ♠
	3 ♠	4 ◇
	?	

Responder holds:

♠ K 10 9 5   ♡ 7   ◇ 10 7 4 3 2   ♣ A 8 2

Responder's values are sound without being exceptional. He would like to make the encouraging move of ascending to 5 ♣ rather than signing off in 4 ♠. Better yet, a bid of 4 ♡ offers encouragement with greater safety.

A player who has indicated a weak hand by giving a negative response to a forcing opening bid may often show second-round control quite safely:

	OPENER	RESPONDER
	2 ♣	2 ◇
	2 ♠	3 ♠
	4 ◇	?

Responder holds:

♠ J 8 4 3   ♡ K 9 3 2   ◇ 7 6 4   ♣ 10 5

Responder should not hesitate to show the king of hearts; if he does not, a slam may be missed. It is true that responder could hold ♡ A and still give a negative response to 2 ♣, but in this sequence the weak hand is more likely to hold a king than an ace and opener should allow for this.

In practice it is usually safe enough for a player to cue-bid any secondary control when he has considerable undisclosed values but no primary control, as in this example:

OPENER	RESPONDER
1 ♣	1 ♡
2 NT	3 ◇
3 ♡	?

Responder holds:

♠ 4   ♡ A Q 10 7 2   ◇ K 10 8 3   ♣ K 10 4

Responder's hand warrants a mild slam try, and he may bid either 3 ♠ or 4 ♣. Very often it is right to cue-bid a king in preference to a singleton, for this may enable partner to attach value to the queen of the suit. Here it is better to save space by bidding 3 ♠, the singleton suit.

The Grand Slam Try

A cue bid that commits the partnership to the 6-level would be pointless if the cue-bidder had no ambition to go beyond a small slam. Any such bid is therefore termed a grand slam try. For example:

OPENER	RESPONDER
1 ♠	3 ♡
4 ♡	5 ♣
5 ◇	5 ♠

The bidding cannot now stop below 6 ♡, so the object of 5 ♠ must be to seek a grand slam. This is the sort of hand the responder may hold:

♠ A 2   ♡ A Q 8 5 3 2   ◇ 5   ♣ A K J 8

After the raise to 4 ♡ it is clear that the final contract will be either 6 ♡ or 7 ♡. Since Blackwood may not reveal whether a vital king is missing, the responder adopts a cue-bidding sequence. Over 5 ♠ the opener is expected to arise in his might and bid 7 ♡ if, in addition to ◇ A, which he has already shown, he holds ♠ K and ♡ K. Partner can hardly be interested in any other cards.

The Advance Cue Bid

When there is no space to raise partner's trump suit and still leave room for a cue bid below the level of game, it may be possible to make an *advance* cue bid—a cue bid in advance of the formal agreement of the trump suit. For example:

OPENER	RESPONDER
1 NT	3 ♠
4 ♣	

The bid of 4 ♣ in a natural sense does not exist in this sequence—opener must either support spades or bid 3 NT. Thus 4 ♣ must mean: "I am supporting your spade call and showing ♣ A on the way, lest you happen to be interested in slam." If responder now bids 4 ♠, that is the end of the matter.

This is the sort of hand where slam is likely to be missed unless the technique of the advance cue bid is employed:

OPENER	RESPONDER
♠ K Q 7 3	♠ A 10 8 6 4 2
♡ A J 2	♡ 5
◇ K 10 7 3	◇ Q J 4
♣ A 8	♣ K 6 3

OPENER	RESPONDER
1 NT	3 ♠
4 ♣ (a)	4 NT (b)
5 ♡	6 ♠
Pass	

(a) Opener has excellent support for his partner's suit, good controls and a ruffing value, so he cue-bids ♣ A.

(b) If opener had simply bid 4 ♠, it would not have been safe for responder to look for slam with this hand. As it is, he credits opener with a maximum and revalues his own hand as at least 15 points, including trump control. Responder is prepared to bid 6 ♠ if partner has two aces.

A second type of advance cue bid is perhaps not quite so easily recognized. Consider the responder's predicament here:

OPENER	RESPONDER
1 ♠	2 ◇
3 ♡	?

Responder holds:

♠ 5   ♡ Q 9 8 6   ◇ Q J 10 7 2   ♣ A J 8

Slam is a distinct possibility, but the responder cannot safely bid 4 NT, for there may be two diamond losers. On the other hand, if he simply raises to 4 ♡ it is most unlikely that opener will be able to continue. A jump to 5 ♡ would indicate the responder's values well enough, but may leave opener stranded if he has two losing clubs. The best call, therefore, is an advance cue bid of 4 ♣. Opener will realize that partner would hardly want to introduce a club suit at this late stage. In any case, whatever the opener bids now, responder continues with 5 ♡ and the scales fall from opener's eyes.

The Blackwood Convention

Gibraltar may crumble, the Rockies may tumble, but Blackwood is likely to remain firmly entrenched as the most popular of all slam conventions. Its great—and sometimes fatal—attraction is its extreme simplicity: over 4 NT the responder bids 5 ♣ with no ace (or with four!), 5 ◇ with one ace, 5 ♡ with two aces, and 5 ♠

with three. If the player who bid 4 NT is interested in a grand slam, he may now bid 5 NT to ask for kings according to the same schedule—6 ♣ for no kings or all four, and so on. The 5 NT inquiry, incidentally, is absolutely *verboten* unless partner's previous bid has established that all four aces are present in the two hands.

The simplicity of the Blackwood convention is such that it tends to be overemployed. A player should bid 4 NT only when three conditions are met:

(1) It must already be clear that the two hands contain enough strength for slam.

(2) There must be no risk that partner's response, when not enough aces are held, will carry the bidding past a safe level.

(3) It must be sufficient to know *how many* aces partner holds rather than *which ones*.

Without doubt, there are many cases where Blackwood works perfectly. Apart from hands of overwhelming strength where only a shortage of aces is likely to keep you out of slam, Blackwood is ideal in this type of hand:

OPENER	RESPONDER
1 ♠	2 ♡
3 ♣	3 ♢
4 ♡	?

♠ Q	♡ K 10 7 6 4 3	♢ J 10 8 6	♣ A 2

Opener has shown great strength and has gone out of his way to indicate that he has no more than one card in diamonds. It is clear that all vital conditions for the use of Blackwood are met. With so little wastage there will surely be few problems in assembling twelve tricks. There is no danger that the response to 4 NT will carry the partnership past a safe level. Finally, any two aces in partner's hand will suffice, as there will not be two quick losers in any suit.

Now for some typical situations where the Blackwood Convention is sometimes misused. Here is a common type of hand where ease of use is apt to lure the inexperienced.

OPENER	RESPONDER
1 ♣	2 ♠
3 ♠	?

Responder holds:

♠ K Q J 5 3   ♡ K 8 4   ◇ A 4   ♣ K 7 2

Because the responder is well endowed with second-round controls, he may be tempted to bid 4 NT. This would be premature, for he has not established the presence of sufficient strength: opener may have a minimum hand offering only a poor play for twelve tricks. The sound move is 4 ◇, permitting opener to clarify his hand.

The requirement that the Blackwood bidder must want to know how many aces partner has, rather than which ones, is often overlooked. In the next hand the troublesome factor is the absence of second-round control in clubs.

OPENER	RESPONDER
1 ♡	2 ♠
3 ◇	3 ♡
4 ♡	?

Responder holds:

♠ A K J 2   ♡ K 10 9 3   ◇ A 5   ♣ Q J 2

In one way this situation is favorable for the use of Blackwood: Opener, by indicating his willingness to stop at 4 ♡, has shown a minimum or near-minimum hand, but the responder has sufficient values to ensure a good play for twelve tricks—and no more than twelve. So far as that goes, it is right for responder to take control by bidding 4 NT. However, if the opener were to respond showing one ace, the responder would not know whether there were two losing clubs. A better bid over 4 ♡ is 5 ◇. After this powerful sequence, opener must come forth with 6 ♡ if he has an opening bid and a club control.

STOPPING AT 5 NT AFTER 4 NT

It can be frustrating to be unable to bid 4 NT for fear of an unfavorable response. On some hands, however, there is a solution. Suppose that you are willing to play 5 NT in the event that your partner has not enough aces for slam. In that case you may bid 4 NT and, if partner's response is unfavorable, continue with *five of a new suit* over this response. Partner—assuming, of course, that he is familiar with this refinement—will then bid 5 NT, which can be passed.

	OPENER	RESPONDER	
	1 ♣	2 ♡	
	4 ♣	?	

Responder holds:

♠ K Q 10   ♡ A Q 9 8 6   ◇ K ♩ J   ♣ 10 2

Opener has shown a solid club suit, so there will be thirteen tricks for the taking if he has three aces. There will be an almost equally easy twelve tricks if he has only two aces. There is just one dark shadow: A bid of 4 NT may elicit the disappointing response of 5 ◇, partner having opened with a solid club suit and ♡ K. Even so, you are willing to bid 4 NT, for over a response of 5 ◇ you intend to bid 5 ♠. This bid of a new suit commands opener to bid 5 NT, which will surely be safe.

BIDDING 4 NT WITH FOUR ACES

There is one very agreeable exception to the principle that you do not use Blackwood unless you want to know how many aces your partner holds. This occurs when you employ the convention to *tell* partner that all four aces are present. For example:

OPENER	RESPONDER
1 ♣	1 ◇
3 ♣	?

Responder holds:

♠ A 8 7 3   ♡ A 10 4   ◇ A 10 8 2   ♣ A 6

After partner's jump rebid in clubs, you are prepared to contract straightaway for 6 ♣—you yourself have not the values to bid more. However, it costs nothing to go through the Blackwood routine, bidding first 4 NT and then 5 NT over the inevitable 5 ♣ response. This tells partner that you have four aces. If partner has, say, seven clubs and all the kings, or K, K-Q and singleton in the side suits, he may be able to bid the grand slam!

A bid of 5 NT by the Blackwood bidder is in fact a guarantee that no ace is missing. Partner is entitled to act on this assumption, and so you never bid 5 NT to ask for kings unless there are four aces in the combined hands. Three aces and a void are not enough!

WHEN 4 NT IS NOT BLACKWOOD

A bid of 4 NT is not always Blackwood, and you can often judge a player's ability by his use of this invaluable bid in a non-conventional sense to suggest a slam in notrump. However, misunderstanding is not by any means unknown and tends to be costly. With a casual partner it is wise to avoid bidding a natural 4 NT in all but the simplest sequences, such as 1 NT-4 NT and 2 NT-4 NT. With a regular partner, it is a sound idea to agree that 4 NT will also be natural when suits have been bid only in a conventional sense, as here:

(1)	OPENER	RESPONDER		(2)	OPENER	RESPONDER
	1 NT	2 ♣			2 ♣	2 NT
	2 ◇	4 NT			4 NT	

In each case 4 NT is natural. Many regular partners also have the understanding that 4 NT is natural even when genuine suits have been bid, provided it is clear that no suit has been agreed as trump. For example:

(3)	OPENER	RESPONDER		(4)	OPENER	RESPONDER
	1 ♠	2 ♣			1 ♠	2 ♡
	3 NT	4 NT			2 NT	3 ◇
					3 NT	4 NT

Again 4 NT is natural. There are, however, two exceptions: Even when no suit has been agreed, 4 NT is still conventional when it represents a *jump* bid over a suit (1 ♠-2 ♡-4 NT), and also when bid by a player who has made a jump shift (1 ♠-3 ♣-3 NT-4 NT).

When Blackwood cannot be used because 4 NT would be natural, it is sometimes possible to use the Gerber Convention instead.

BLACKWOOD IN COMPETITION

Sometimes the opponents will attempt to interfere with the mechanism of a Blackwood sequence, as here:

OPENER	OPPONENT	RESPONDER	OPPONENT
1 ♡	Pass	3 ♡	4 ◇
4 NT	5 ◇	?	

A method of coping with this situation is recommended by Easley Blackwood, inventor of the convention: The responder bids one step up for every ace he holds. Thus 5 ♡ in the sequence above would show one ace, 5 ♠ would show two aces, and so on. However, the responder is allowed some discretion, and a pass would say: "Either I have no ace or the opponents' bidding has made it unwise to show how many I have." A double is natural.

Experts have devised a more sophisticated way to stop the opponents from jamming the Blackwood exchanges. Actually, there are two variants of the same idea. One is called DOPI—an acronym for Double with 0 aces, Pass with 1. The other, called DIPO, simply reverses the two meanings. Using either method, a bid in the next available suit shows two aces. These methods are simple enough to add accuracy to your slam bidding at the small cost of burdening yourself with a self-checking mnemonic. As between the two variants, there is this to be said for DOPI: If you double with no ace, there is less chance that your action will cost a forgetful partnership a slam.

SHOWING A VOID SUIT

As Blackwood tells you only how many aces are present, rather than which ones, a player who is void in a suit usually does better to employ cue bids rather than bid 4 NT. However, it is possible for the *responder* to 4 NT to show a void suit. For obvious reasons a void may not be counted as an ace, and instead there is a special set of responses at the 6-level to show voids. The scheme proposed by Easley Blackwood is that you bid the right suit to show the number of aces held, but at the 6-level instead of the 5-level. Thus:

OPENER	RESPONDER
1 ♠	2 ♡
3 ♣	3 ♡
4 ♡	4 NT
6 ♡	

However, he cautions that the responder to 4 NT should take this action only when the void is in a suit that the Blackwood bidder may be expected to identify. In the foregoing sequence, opener is showing two aces and a void. Here, with the gray cells functioning smoothly, it is possible to work out where the opener's void is, since he has bid two suits and supported a third.

KEY-CARD BLACKWOOD

Most attempts to improve on Blackwood are fairly trivial in comparison with the original convention. One variation that has practical merit is Key-card Blackwood, which recognizes the value of the king of trumps by treating it as a fifth ace. The responses to 4 NT now become:

5 ♣	No 'ace' or four
5 ♦	One 'ace' or five
5 ♥	Two 'aces'
5 ♠	Three 'aces'

A subsequent bid of 5 NT asks for kings to be shown in the normal fashion. Of course, the king of trumps is *not* shown a second time.

The following is the sort of hand in which Key-card Black-wood earns its keep.

OPENER	RESPONDER
♠ Q J 8 6 5	♠ 10 9 7 2
♥ 4	♥ A Q 3
♦ A K Q 10	♦ 8 6
♣ K Q 10	♣ A J 8 4

OPENER	RESPONDER
1 ♠	3 ♠
4 ♦	4 ♥
4 NT	5 ♥
?	

Playing standard Blackwood, opener may be tempted to bid a slam, which is hard to make. Playing the Key-card version, he knows that either two aces are missing or one ace and the king of trumps. A slam, at the very best, will depend on a finesse, so opener signs off in 5 ♠.

Before leaving the subject I have one more suggestion to offer. If you suspect that you, like many players, may be overworking the Blackwood Convention, you should try the effect of renouncing it altogether for three or four sessions. Like a man deprived of one of his senses, you will begin to develop the others more fully, and you may well be delighted to find how useful such alternative weapons as cue bids can be. When you resume the use of Blackwood it will have taken its proper place in the scheme of things.

The Gerber Convention

The need for this ace-finding device does not often occur, but it plugs a gap that arises when partner's last bid was in notrump and the Blackwood Convention cannot be used. In such a case a jump to 4 ♣ (provided this suit has not been previously mentioned) is Gerber, asking for aces according to the familiar "step" system. The responses are: 4 ◇—no ace or four aces; 4 ♡—one ace; 4 ♠—two aces; 4 NT—three aces. The 4 ♣ bidder may then bid 5 ♣ to ask for kings.

The following are sequences in which 4 ♣ would be Gerber:

(1)	OPENER	RESPONDER		(2)	OPENER	RESPONDER
	1 NT	4 ♣			2 NT	4 ♣

(3)	OPENER	RESPONDER		(4)	OPENER	RESPONDER
	1 ♡	2 NT			1 ♡	1 ♠
	4 ♣				2 NT	4 ♣

8

Coping with Intervention

♠ ♡ ◇ ♣

The Forcing Pass—Cue-Bidding the Opponent's Suit—"Unusual" Notrump by the Opening Side—Doubles by a Player Who Has Opened

Many players consider it good tactics, when their opponents appear to have the stronger hands, to intervene readily and push the bidding as high as they dare. Players who favor these tactics sometimes overstep the mark in perilous fashion, but all the same it is very necessary that you have the best scheme of defense against them.

This scheme begins with certain commonsense adjustments to the standard responses and rebids. For example, when your partner opens with a bid of one and there is an overcall, you no longer scrape up a "courtesy" response with a borderline hand. If you would have been uncertain whether to bid or pass without the overcall, then of course you pass. In the same way, when you have opened with a minimum or near-minimum, you do not normally rebid freely in competition, as here again your partner is still at the table. In all such situations you follow the sound principle that when one has nothing to say, one should say nothing.

However, it does not follow that you always bid cautiously in competition. When you have found a fit you follow the opposite tack, raising to the higher level whenever there is a close decision. Suppose you are the opener in the following example:

OPENER	OPPONENT	RESPONDER	OPPONENT
1 ♣	Pass	1 ♡	2 ♠ (weak)
?			

Opener holds:

♠ A 4   ♡ K 10 9 3   ◇ K 3   ♣ A Q 10 8 4

With no intervention you might be undecided whether to raise to 3 ♡ or 4 ♡ with this hand. As it is, you should bid 4 ♡, in line with the principle of selecting the stronger bid when you have a fit with partner. In all competitive situations *the more you have in your partner's suit the more it will pay your side to play the hand*.

However, the general philosophy of competitive bidding is not really the subject of this chapter—we are concerned more specifically with powerhouse auctions. Attempts to obstruct these are not all honey, for an opponent who intervenes presents you with options that you would not otherwise have enjoyed. You may be able to double for penalty or, in a different situation, for takeout. You may be able to make a forcing pass, which is a very useful maneuver, or a cue bid in the opponent's suit. Sometimes, too, it is possible to extend the principle of the Unusual Notrump, which is normally used by the defending side, in order to invite partner to choose a suit. Few players use these competitive devices to the full, especially the forcing pass.

The Forcing Pass

A pass, even when dignified by a special name, may seem a feeble counter to an opponent who ventures to interfere with your powerhouse auction. However, it represents a valuable addition to the range of calls, and it deserves to be fully exploited. Consider this sequence:

OPENER	OPPONENT	RESPONDER	OPPONENT
2 ♣	Pass	2 ◇	2 ♠
?			

Opener's side is vulnerable and opener holds:

♠ A 4 2   ♡ A K J   ◇ A K 9 6   ♣ K Q J

Opener started out with the intention of rebidding this hand at
3 NT, and he could still do so. However, he does not much like the
look of the single spade guard, so he may pass and wait to hear from
partner. Responder may not pass 2 ♠, under penalty of boiling in
oil: Once the bidding has been opened with 2 ♣ you do not allow
opponents to play the hand undoubled. Here, in fact, opener has
gained a round of bidding; he can raise a call of 3 ♡ or 3 ◇ and bid
3 NT over 3 ♣, with the additional possibility of defending against
2 ♠ doubled if responder has a suitable hand.
    A forcing pass may be made in any sequence where the last bid
by the partnership was forcing. Thus:

OPENER	OPPONENT	RESPONDER	OPPONENT
1 NT	Pass	3 ♡	3 ♠
?			

Opener's side is vulnerable and opener holds:

♠ Q J 7   ♡ A 7 2   ◇ A Q 5   ♣ K J 10 6

Without the butt-in, opener might have considered bidding
either 3 NT or 4 ♡. The overcall provides him with a third choice,
a forcing pass, and this in fact will be better, allowing the next move

to come from partner. Suppose the responder holds either of these hands:

(1) ♠ 8 3 2   ♡ K Q J 6 4   ◇ 9 7 6   ♣ A 4
(2) ♠ 6   ♡ K J 9 5 4   ◇ K J 3   ♣ Q 9 8 3

With the first hand the responder can see the obvious possibility of a damaging spade ruff if the hand is played at a contract of 4 ♡. He therefore bids 3 NT, hoping there will be nine running tricks. Opener, of course, will not pass 3 NT in this sequence unless he has a spade guard.

With (2) the responder can be confident that 3 NT is not the right contract. If it were, the opener would either have bid it already or have doubled 3 ♠. Moreover, responder's own lack of aces and the broken quality of his five-card suit argue against there being nine running tricks. Responder therefore bids 4 ♡. Note that if opener had not availed himself of a forcing pass, the wrong contract might have been reached with either of these hands.

The use of the forcing pass may be extended by experienced players to situations where the last bid by the partnership is not by definition forcing, but where the two partners have shown so much strength that they could not conceivably be willing to allow opponents to play the hand undoubled.

OPENER	OPPONENT	RESPONDER	OPPONENT
1 ♣	Pass	1 ♡	1 ♠
1 NT	Pass	3 ♡	Pass
4 ♡	4 ♠	?	

Suppose that you are the responder. Your side is vulnerable and you hold:

♠ 7   ♡ K Q 10 8 4 3   ◇ K Q 5   ♣ J 6 2

This is not easy. Perhaps you can make 5 ♡; perhaps the best you can do is double 4 ♠. Fortunately you can pass the decision to your partner, who will treat this pass as forcing because it is clear that you and he have so much in high cards that you would not be willing to allow the opponents to play the hand undoubled.

Then there are some gray areas where it is not clear whether or not a pass, at a high level, will be forcing. For example, suppose that your side has the balance of strength, but this strength consists largely of distributional values. In such cases, it may not be obvious who, if anyone, is saving against whom—maybe both sides can make their contract. Here you are the opener:

OPENER	OPPONENT	RESPONDER	OPPONENT
1 ♠	4 ♡	4 ♠	5 ♡
?			

Opener holds:

♠ K Q 8 5 3   ♡ 8   ◇ A J 4   ♣ K J 8 2

On the whole yours is an attacking type of hand. Against that is the fact that your partner may have been placed under strong pressure by the 4 ♡ overcall. It may be that he has less spade support and more defensive strength than is usual for a raise to four. Because you cannot tell whether to double or bid 5 ♠, you should pass. Now your partner should take some action. Since your side is vulnerable, he should assume that the opening bid is sound, with three likely defensive tricks. The least he can do, therefore, is to double.

Not every pass over a high-level intervention is forcing. There are some hands where the opening side, even after it has reached game, may have to bow the knee. In this auction the defending side is vulnerable:

OPENER	OPPONENT	RESPONDER	OPPONENT
1 ♡	1 ♠	4 ♡	4 ♠
?			

Opener holds:

♠ 8 3   ♡ K J 10 7 3   ◊ A Q 8   ♣ Q 10 5

The responder may have no real defensive strength, and there
is nothing in the bidding to suggest that the opponents cannot make
4 ♠. Therefore a pass by opener is not forcing.

THE FORCING PASS AT SLAM LEVEL

Sometimes the choice is between doubling a sacrifice at slam
level or risking a grand slam.

OPENER	OPPONENT	RESPONDER	OPPONENT
1 ♣	Pass	1 ◊	1 ♡
2 ♠	4 ♡	4 ♠	5 ♡
6 ♠	Pass	Pass	7 ♡
?			

Your side is vulnerable and you hold:

♠ A Q 9 5 2   ♡ A 6   ◊ 9   ♣ A K Q 10 3

The vital consideration is not that a pass will be forcing, which
is obvious, but that it will guarantee first-round control of the enemy
suit. Without control of this suit *you would have to double 7 ♡*, to
warn partner against bidding 7 ♠. (The double would not necessarily *prevent* your partner from bidding the grand slam if he himself
happened to have control of the enemy suit plus suitable key cards.)
The principle here is that when *the strong partner* passes an obvious

sacrificial bid at the 7-level, he is showing control and inviting a grand slam. Even with this reassurance, partner is not expected to bid seven unless he has favorable key cards—after all, the partnership was previously willing to stop at six. In this example the responder would not bid 7 ♠ unless he held control of his own suit and a key card in the trump suit—in other words, ◇ A and ♠ K.

Clearly this type of pass should not be used with the accident-prone. At rubber bridge, even if you are not playing with the kind of partner who is apt to run into a tidal wave in the middle of the Sahara Desert, you would be much more inclined to double the opponents and take the short money. At duplicate, however, the odds required for a grand slam must be adjusted when the non-vulnerable opponents sacrifice. It is sometimes better to allow yourself to be pushed into a risky grand slam than to accept a limited penalty.

Cue-Bidding the Opponent's Suit

The cue bid in the opponent's suit is a rather different animal from the ace-showing cue bid described in the previous chapter. It is used *to create a forcing situation*, not necessarily to show a control. It can be used both by the defending side and by the opening side. Here we are concerned with its use by the opening side, a role in which it has become vital because of a change of practice in recent years.

One of the earliest ideas in contract bridge was that a bid in a suit previously bid by an opponent should be based on first-round control of this suit—the ace or void—with strong support for partner's suit. This cue bid showed the values for at least a game and indicated a strong interest in slam. Thus:

OPENER	OPPONENT	RESPONDER	OPPONENT
1 ♡	1 ♠	2 ♠	

A typical hand for responder would be:

♠ A   ♡ K Q 10 4   ◇ K J 8 5 2   ♣ A 10 2

Undoubtedly this is very pleasant, and some players still use the cue bid in this sense. But, as we all know, such hands do not come along too often, and when they do this is not the only way of coping with them. Therefore the more modern practice, which is strongly recommended, is to use the cue bid as a general-purpose force in any hand where it is clear that game-going values are present and no sound natural bid is available. There are many hands where the use of the cue bid in this sense is almost a necessity. Here the cue bid is used by opener.

OPENER	OPPONENT	RESPONDER	OPPONENT
1 ♡	2 ♣	2 ◇	Pass
?			

Opener holds:

♠ A K 5   ♡ A Q 8 5 3   ◇ A 2   ♣ J 7 4

Had there been no butt-in, the natural rebid would have been 3 NT, taking a chance on the club suit. As it is, there is no satisfactory natural bid. Opener does not want to risk falling short of game, so he bids 3 ♣. This says nothing about his club holding or about his holding in partner's suit. The message is simply that game is expected to be there in some denomination or other. Partner is invited to clarify his hand, bidding 3 NT with a club guard, showing heart support or a secondary spade suit, or rebidding his own suit.

The cue bid may be employed by either player as a general-purpose force. No fixed level of strength is needed. The essential requirement is that there should be game-going values in the combined hands. In the next example the opener employs the cue bid with a less strong hand because his partner has shown good values.

OPENER	OPPONENT	RESPONDER	OPPONENT
1 ♣	1 ♠	2 ♡	Pass
2 ♠			

Opener holds:

♠ 7 6 4   ♡ Q 2   ◇ A 10 5   ♣ A K Q J 4

Over partner's strong response a simple rebid of 3 ♣ does not fill the bill, for this would be consistent with a minimum opening hand. Opener is willing to play in 3 NT if partner has a spade guard, in 4 ♡ (possibly 5 ♣) if he hasn't.

A responder who is not strong enough to force initially may do so when his partner makes an encouraging rebid.

OPENER	OPPONENT	RESPONDER	OPPONENT
1 ♠	2 ♡	Pass	Pass
3 ♣	Pass	3 ♡	

Responder holds:

♠ J 4   ♡ 8 5 2   ◇ A 7 6 4 3   ♣ Q J 5

The opener has shown a powerful two-suited hand and the responder should feel mightily encouraged by the turn of events. The best way to convey that he is prepared for a game contract in either spades, clubs or notrump is by bidding 3 ♡.

Bridge theorists are most reluctant to accept the defeatist view that you cannot have your cake and eat it as well. Thus a way has been found to continue to portray the very strong type of hand with enormous support for partner and control of the enemy suit—the sort of hand for which the use of the cue bid was formerly reserved. The procedure now is that you make a *jump* bid in the opponent's suit, as follows:

OPENER	OPPONENT	RESPONDER	OPPONENT
1 ♠	2 ♣	4 ♣	

Responder holds:

♠ K Q 10 4 2   ♡ A K 7   ◊ J 10 4   ♣ A 5

With this rockcrusher a bid of 4 ♠ is not to be contemplated; nor is a Blackwood bid of 4 NT a solution, for there is no indication whether partner has a strong or weak opening. The jump bid in the opponent's suit, an otherwise idle bid, shows this type of hand.

Finally, it is possible to distinguish a strong hand with powerful trump support but no control in the enemy suit.

OPENER	OPPONENT	RESPONDER	OPPONENT
1 ♡	1 ♠	?	

Responder holds:

♠ 9 4   ♡ A Q 10 5 4   ◊ K 10 8 3   ♣ A J

Had there been no butt-in, responder might have attempted to show this hand by responding in diamonds and later supporting hearts strongly. In a contested auction such a sequence is unattractive, for you may never succeed in completing the picture of your hand. Instead, it is better to announce this strength immediately by bidding 2 ♠. Partner will not know that you are forcing on the strength of a powerful heart holding. But when you later support hearts at every turn, the essential message will come through. There will also be a negative inference that you do not have ♠ A, as you did not bid 3 ♠ over 1 ♠.

"Unusual" Notrump by the Opening Side

The reader may be familiar with the Unusual Notrump Convention. One of several major contributions by Alvin Roth, it has won wide acceptance by tournament players. Its purpose is to enable a defender to contest the bidding with a two-suited hand, usually in the minor suits.

A direct bid of 2 NT over an opponent's 1 ♠ or 1 ♡ is treated as "unusual," suggesting at least 5-5 in clubs and diamonds. (With a genuine 2 NT call, you double first.) The 2 NT bid is also "unusual" in any situation where it cannot logically be genuine, such as this:

SOUTH	WEST	NORTH	EAST
1 ♡	Pass	2 ♡	Pass
Pass	2 NT		

West clearly wants partner to bid one of the minor suits, although here, where the Unusual Notrump is used as a balancing move, the distributional pattern may be less strongly marked than in the direct position.

I believe it was Alan Truscott who first suggested in a series of magazine articles that the Unusual Notrump, devised for use by the defenders, could profitably be employed by the opening side when a bid of notrump cannot logically be natural. In this example the defenders are sacrificing in spades and have placed the responder in some difficulty:

OPENER	OPPONENT	RESPONDER	OPPONENT
1 ♡	1 ♠	2 ♣	4 ♠
Pass	Pass	?	

The opening side is vulnerable and the responder holds:

♠ 6   ♡ Q 9 4   ◇ A Q 5   ♣ K J 10 5 4 3

A double of 4 ♠ may not be very profitable, and responder would rather take his chances in 5 ♣ or 5 ♡. He cannot tell which suit will be better, so he bids 4 NT, a very neat way of inviting partner to choose. Note that it must be clear that the notrump bidder cannot want to play the hand in notrump. This means in practice that only bids of 4 NT and 5 NT are "unusual," and then only when they cannot be confused with Blackwood.

It is sometimes possible to invite partner to choose between two suits when only one has actually been mentioned! In this example you are the responder and partner is relying on your deductive powers.

OPENER	OPPONENT	RESPONDER	OPPONENT
2 ♣ (a)	2 ♡	Pass	4 ♡
5 ♣	5 ♡	Pass	Pass
5 NT	Pass	?	

(a) Artificial

Responder holds:

♠ 10 7 6 3   ♡ 8 4 2   ◇ J 9 8 4 2   ♣ 2

Clearly you are being invited to choose between clubs and some secondary suit. If opener held a spade suit it would have been natural to bid this over 5 ♡, so the obvious call for you to make now is 6 ◇. Opener's hand is probably something like this:

♠ A 8   ♡ 6   ◇ A K Q 3   ♣ A K J 9 7 4

Such an advanced use of the Unusual Notrump calls for straight thinking, but it certainly helps reduce the element of guesswork.

Doubles by a Player
Who Has Opened

Just as the Unusual Notrump, invented for use by the defenders, can be helpful to the opening side, so too is the takeout double a valuable resource for a player with a strong opening hand:

OPENER	OPPONENT	RESPONDER	OPPONENT
1 ♠	2 ◊	Pass	Pass
?			

Opener holds:

♠ A K J 8 2   ♡ Q 10 7   ◊ 6   ♣ A Q 10 5

Opener does not wish to sell out, for the responder has been prevented from calling at the one-level and may well have some values. A bid of 2 ♠ or 3 ♣ might hit partner's weakness or bypass a suitable contract in hearts. A double is recommended because it keeps all options open—including a penalty pass by partner if his only strength is in diamonds. Note that this double conforms to the standard definition for a normal takeout double: "A double made at the first opportunity of doubling and when partner has not made a bid."

In the next example the double suggests a still stronger hand because responder has denied the ability to bid at the one-level.

OPENER	OPPONENT	RESPONDER	OPPONENT
1 ♡	Pass	Pass	2 ◊
Double			

Opener holds:

♠ A 8 3   ♡ A Q J 7 4   ◊ 6   ♣ A K 10 7

Despite responder's pass, it is likely that the hand belongs to the opening side. A double is once again the most comprehensive move.

When a player has previously shown weakness, he may be able to respond to a double with a cue bid.

OPENER	OPPONENT	RESPONDER	OPPONENT
1 ♡	2 ◊	Pass	Pass
Double	Pass	?	

Responder holds:

♠ 10 9 5 3   ♡ Q 4   ◊ 7 6 5 2   ♣ A Q 3

Considering the bidding, this is a very fine hand indeed. The only bid that does it justice is 3 ◊.

9

Powerhouse Overcalls

♠ ♡ ◇ ♣

The Direct Cue Bid—The 1 NT Overcall—The Takeout Double—The Jump Overcall— Countering a Preempt—Entering at the 4-Level

So far we have blithely assumed that the player with a powerhouse hand has enjoyed a clear run, or has at least been permitted to open the bidding in suitable style. However, sometimes the opponents, either from antisocial motives or in the erroneous belief that this is their hand, may open in front of you. It is well to recognize that this will often make it harder to reach the right contract.

The standard methods of unveiling a strong hand when opponents have opened with a bid of one are by means of a direct cue bid, an overcall of 1 NT, a double or a jump overcall. (It will be noted that the *simple* overcall is not in this list. This call is a workhorse for dealing with moderate to average hands, and its upper limit of strength is normally that of a sound minimum opening bid.) These calls are also employed against opening 3-bids and against weak 2-bids. Then there are the situations, which require especially good judgment, where one has to enter at a high level after an opening 4-bid or after an opposing sequence such as 1 ♡-4 ♡.

The Direct Cue Bid

When you cue-bid the opener's suit at the first opportunity you are proclaiming that your strength, figuratively speaking, is as the strength of ten—almost equal to an opening 2-bid. Except in certain sequences, which will be noted later, partner may not pass until a game is reached or the opponents have been doubled for penalty.

The same is true when you cue-bid *the responder's* suit at the first opportunity and your partner has not bid. Thus:

OPPONENT	PARTNER	OPPONENT	YOU
1 ♣	Pass	1 ♡	2 ♡

Here also you are, in theory, showing a game-going hand. In practice a degree of optimism is allowed—indeed, is encouraged. If you were to wait until you held a sure game in your own hand, you might hardly ever use this bid in your whole life. It is wrong to set such strict standards for any bid that it becomes of little practical use.

Suppose there is an opening bid of 1 ♠ on your right and you have this hand:

♠ 5   ♡ A 9 8 6   ◇ A   ♣ A K Q J 8 5 2

If partner has a spade guard you can make 3 NT. If he has any four cards in hearts, the chances are that you can make game in this suit. Then there is the possibility of a game in clubs. Therefore you should make a direct cue bid of 2 ♠, even though it is clear that you will not make game if partner is busted. Consider the alternatives. If you overcall with 3 ♣, this will in all probability close the auction; if you double for takeout and next hand bids, say, 2 ♠, your partner will not necessarily hie himself into notrump with ♠ Q-J-x and nothing much else. In general, when you have a hand as promising as this, you permit yourself to be moved by the Biblical principle, "If the trumpet give an uncertain sound, who shall gird himself to the fray?"

The direct cue bid is usually better than a double when you have a very distributional type of hand, a pronounced one-suiter or two-suiter with perhaps a void in opener's suit. If you double with such a hand and your partner decides to pass for penalty, you may get a catastrophic result. In the following hands you would be justified in bidding 2 ♡ over an opening 1 ♡ :

(1) ♠ A K Q 10 8 5 3 2 ♡ 8 ◇ 3 2 ♣ A K
(2) ♠ A Q ♡ — ◇ A J 10 3 ♣ A K 10 9 8 6 4
(3) ♠ A Q J 10 5 ♡ 7 ◇ 10 ♣ A K Q 10 8 2

With (1) you could bid 4 ♠ straightaway, and indeed if you held a little less in high cards this would be the right course. As it is, a cue bid of 2 ♡, to be followed by 4 ♠, is preferred. Then, if there is further competitive bidding, your partner will know that the opponents are saving against you and not you against them.

Hand (2) is too strong for a bid of 3 ♣, while a double would be unsatisfactory since (a) partner might expect better support for spades and (b) if partner were to pass a double for penalty, the result would almost surely be poor.

With (3) you bid 2 ♡, hoping to be able to bid clubs first and then spades. However, if the opponents crowd the auction you are willing, if necessary, to hide the clubs and take your chances in 4 ♠.

You may encounter some players who insist on having first-round control of the enemy suit before making a direct cue bid. This is very poor policy indeed, for it limits still further the use of a bid that already occurs infrequently. It has almost no compensating virtue because when the opponents open with a bid of one, you very seldom entertain any serious expectation of making a slam, whether you have control of their suit or not. As a matter of fact, in tournament bridge many players no longer use the direct cue bid on any kind of strong hand, relying instead on the takeout double. These players prefer to put the direct cue bid to what they consider a more productive use, a popular example being the Michaels Cue Bid.

THE MICHAELS CUE BID

The reader will have noted that in some of the previous examples the use of a takeout double is not ideal, although it is not altogether impracticable. Accepting the disadvantage of the double on that type of hand, which after all is relatively infrequent, many players double on all strong hands and use the direct cue bid for more modest two-suited hands that are hard to express with a normal overcall or takeout double. The strength of this cue bid depends on vulnerability, and the type of hand shown depends on whether the cue bid is in a minor or a major suit.

Over 1 ♣ or 1 ◇: A direct cue bid shows at least 5-4 in the major suits (many players require 5-5) with a range of 6-11 points in high cards.

♠ K 7 6 4 2   ♡ A J 10 5   ◇ J 3   ♣ 9 2

This hand is suitable for 2 ♣ over 1 ♣, or 2 ◇ over 1 ◇, at equal vulnerability. At unfavorable vulnerability, a more freakish distribution is required.

Over 1 ♡ or 1 ♠: The cue bid shows a hand of unlimited strength with five cards in the unbid major and an unspecified minor suit.

In response the partner will usually bid the full value of his hand if he has a fit in the major suit. If he does not fit the major suit, he may bid 2 NT to ask for the cue-bidder's minor.

RESPONDING TO A DIRECT CUE BID

When you are responding to a direct cue bid (the rockcrusher bid, not the Michaels cue bid variety) and are fortunate enough to possess some appreciable values, you do not necessarily have to show these at once, as you would in response to a double. Your partner may not pass a simple response, and thus there will be a further chance to display your wares. Also, your partner's hand is to some extent an unknown quantity, and you may not immediately be able to tell how much your hand is worth in support. In general, therefore, the proper order of business is first to see how the hands fit and then, on the second round, to express the value of the responding hand. The bidding goes:

OPPONENT	PARTNER	OPPONENT	YOU
1 ◇	2 ◇	Pass	?

You hold:

(1) ♠ K 9 8 6 4 3   ♡ 2   ◇ Q 4 3   ♣ J 7 3
(2) ♠ J 9 5 2   ♡ 7 3   ◇ K Q 10   ♣ 9 8 4 2
(3) ♠ K 4 2   ♡ Q 7 3   ◇ 9 5 4   ♣ A 10 8 4

In (1) you may think with such a promising hand that everything is for the best in this best of possible worlds and that some form of highly enthusiastic response is in order. A moment's reflection, however, tells you that your partner's suit is almost certainly hearts and that your hand may not in fact be worth very much. You therefore start with a quiet 2 ♠. Over the expected 3 ♡ rebid from partner you may consider whether to bid 3 NT; but in fact it will be better to rebid the spades, for partner is more likely to have, say, A-x of this suit than to be willing to contemplate a contract of 3 NT.

With (2) you should respond 2 NT, for your diamonds are an important feature. You may be able to bid spades on the next round, which will make it even plainer that you have a sound diamond guard since you did not bid spades initially. If you were to reverse this procedure, your partner would not be able to repose such confidence in your diamond holding.

Hand (3) must be enormous, no matter what type of hand your partner's cue bid is based on. Still, you should start quietly with 3 ♣. Partner will no doubt bid 3 ♡ or 3 ♠, and now nothing less than a raise to five will do justice to your hand. With a slightly weaker hand you might respond with 3 ◇, signifying that you were prepared for any contract. Once having shown strength by means of this responsive cue bid, you would leave partner to make the running.

It is possible in some sequences to stop short of game after a direct cue bid. In these examples you have the responding hand:

(1)	OPPONENT	PARTNER	OPPONENT	YOU
	1 ♣	2 ♣	Pass	2 ♡
	Pass	2 ♠	Pass	3 ◇
	Pass	3 ♠	Pass	?

With a trickless hand you may pass, for if partner had game in his own hand he would have jumped to 4 ♠.

In the next sequence your partner, with the big hand, is the player who may pass your next bid.

(2)	OPPONENT	PARTNER	OPPONENT	YOU
	1 ♣	2 ♣	Pass	2 ◇
	Pass	2 ♠	Pass	3 ◇
	Pass	3 ♡	Pass	?

You may not pass 3 ♡, but if you can do no more than bid 3 ♠ your partner may pass this call. Therefore, with as much as one trick in your hand, you should jump to 4 ♠. In effect, the direct cue bid is not an unswerving demand for game but is "forcing to sign-off," as the expression goes.

The 1 NT Overcall

1 NT directly over an opponent's bid shows the same strength as a 1 NT opening, 16-18 points. However, there is not quite the same insistence on having a balanced hand pattern. Such a strong hand as this is, by and large, unsuitable for a simple overcall in a suit. 1 NT therefore has to do duty in some rather offbeat hand patterns where, for one reason or another, you cannot make a take-out double. Thus you might well decide to bid 1 NT over 1 ♠ with the following hands as well as with the classic balanced type of hand.

(1) ♠ A Q 8   ♡ J   ◇ K 9 7 6 3   ♣ A K 8 3
(2) ♠ A K 3 2   ♡ Q 7   ◇ K 4   ♣ K J 8 6 2

There are disadvantages in any call, including a trap pass, but an overcall of 1 NT is as good as anything.

RESPONDING TO THE 1 NT OVERCALL

After a 1 NT overcall some partnerships use the Stayman Convention, just as if there had been no opening bid. A more widely used method of exploration, however, is to cue-bid opener's suit.

OPPONENT	PARTNER	OPPONENT	YOU
1 ◇	1 NT	Pass	2 ◇

This cue bid asks the 1 NT overcaller to show a four-card major or to bid 2 NT. If, in the same sequence, you were to bid 2 ♣, 2 ♡ or 2 ♠ over 1 NT, this would be a sign-off.

The Takeout Double

The use of the takeout double is a large subject that is covered comprehensively in the Prentice-Hall Contract Bridge Series.* However, it is mentioned here for the sake of completeness, and to show how it fits in with the other ways of entering the auction with a strong hand.

First, it is essential to know when a double is for takeout and when it is for penalty. Aside from doubles on certain moderate hands in balancing situations, with which we are not concerned, the following definition is comprehensive: A double of a suit below the game level is for takeout if made at the first opportunity of doubling and when partner has not made a call.

*Doubles for Takeout, Penalties and Profit, by Robert B. Ewen.

In the accepted theory of the takeout double there are two types:

1. Doubles on hands of moderate high-card strength —normally not more than about 15 points. For this type of double there are certain safety requirements: The doubler must have support, or at least tolerance, for the unbid suits, and especially for any unbid major suit. The more moderate his hand, the more stringently these requirements are applied. With a hand in this minimum range of strength, the doubler does not normally intend to bid again if his partner can make no more than a simple response to the double.

2. Doubles on hands of good high card strength—16 points or more.

Because this is a book about powerhouse hands, we are concerned more with this second type of double. Now you may double not only with the classic three-suited hand but with almost any unbalanced pattern. The main exception is that you do not double when your hand is suitable for an intermediate jump overcall (discussed later in this chapter) that is more immediately descriptive. You double also on all *balanced* hands too strong for 1 NT.

The reason you may double liberally on these strong unbalanced patterns is that you intend to continue with a developing bid on the second round, which hopefully will clear up your distribution.

For example, when you double and then take out your partner's response into another suit, you indicate that you lack support for your partner's suit, that your own suit is of at least five cards and that your high-card strength is above the minimum. This adds up to quite a comprehensive description. Suppose the player on your right opens with 1 ♡ and you hold:

♠ A K 9 8 4 2   ♡ 7 2   ◇ A K 5   ♣ A 6

You have about one ace too many for an immediate bid of 2 ♠, so you double, intending to bid 2 ♠—strong but not forcing—over a response of 2 ◇ or 2 ♣.

When a player doubles and takes out his partner's response into a *minor* suit, there is always a strong hint that he has four cards in an

unbid major suit; otherwise he might have bid the minor suit in the
first place.

♠ J 10 4 2   ♡ A   ◇ A K Q 9 7 3   ♣ Q 6

Over an opponent's 1 ♡, your first inclination may be to overcall with 3 ◇, but a double is better as partner may have a four-card
spade suit. It tends to be right to double on any strong unbalanced
hand with four cards in the unbid major suit; if you start with a jump
overcall your partner will seldom venture to introduce a weak four-
card suit from his side of the table. Here, if partner responds in
clubs, you simply bid diamonds at the lowest level.

This is an example of a takeout double on a balanced hand:

♠ A J 4   ♡ A Q 6   ◇ A J 2   ♣ K J 5 3

This is a notrump type hand, but too strong for 1 NT. You
therefore double any suit opening and bid notrump at the minimum
level on the next round, showing 19-21 points. There are two
reasons why you do not overcall on the first round with 2 NT. First,
many players treat this call as "unusual," showing length in the
minor suits. Secondly, to double first is safer, as you may be able to
play the hand at the level of 1 NT.

RESPONDING TO A DOUBLE

The scheme of responses is well established: You may not
pass, of course, save when your holding in the suit doubled is so
strong that your most profitable course is to pass for penalties. In
responding to a double you try to indicate the strength of your hand
as well as your best suit. This is necessary because a takeout double
does not promise that the doubler will bid again over a minimum
response. Indeed, even a jump response to a double, although
highly encouraging, does not bind the doubler if he has a complete

minimum. When you want to be sure the doubler will not pass, you must cue bid the opponent's suit.

The use of point count is never an exact science even in uncontested auctions. Still less is it so when responding to a double; but nevertheless it is a guide. The doubler is expected to hold some support for any unbid suit, so the responder may value his hand on the basis that some fit exists Suppose you are the responder here:

OPPONENT	PARTNER	OPPONENT	YOU
1 ♠	Double	2 ♠	?

You hold:

♠ 10 4 3   ♡ Q 7 6 4 2   ◇ A K 6 3   ♣ 8

You intend to respond in hearts, of course. The doubler is presumed to hold support for the unbid major suit (or extra strength), so in valuing your hand you may include "support" points, bringing your count to 12. Moreover, with the likelihood of nine trumps in the combined hands, you may add another point for trump control. Since the doubler is expected to have opening values, already this tells you that you should bid 4 ♡ rather than three. In addition you can be sure that the hands are likely to fit extremely well since you have no points in spades.

When your partner doubles a minor suit, you should not rely too heavily on the likelihood that he holds primary support for both major suits. But still you may make some addition to your high-card points, to take into account the chance that there will be a fit. Valuing your hand in this way, here is the basic scheme of responses to a double, after a pass by third hand:

With 13 points or more: Either jump straight to game or cue-bid the opponent's suit.

With 9 to 12 points: Make a jump response in your best suit, giving preference to a four-card major suit over a four-card or five-card minor. This response is not forcing.

With 0 to 8 points: Make a minimum response in a suit, still giving preference to a major suit and aiming in general to find a fit at the lowest level.

There are two types of response that do not slot neatly into these categories. First is the response of 1 NT, which in theory is constructive and may show from about 6 to as many as 9 or 10 points in high cards, with a guard in the opponent's suit, of course. In practice this bid sometimes has to be employed, by force of circumstances, with a weaker hand.

OPPONENT	PARTNER	OPPONENT	YOU
1 ♠	Double	Pass	?

You hold:

♠ Q J 9 3   ♡ 7 6 2   ◇ 8 5 4   ♣ Q 9 6

To bid anything but 1 NT with this hand would be a worse crime than overstating the strength of your hand by a point. If partner raises, you may be too high for comfort, but at least you will be in the right strain.

The second type of response that cuts across the normal guide lines is the response in competition. This is just commonsense, of course. If, without the competition, you would have had only just about enough for a jump response, then over a bid by third hand you make a simple response, and so on.

OPPONENT	PARTNER	OPPONENT	YOU
1 ♡	Double	2 ♡	?

You hold:

♠ K 7 5 3   ♡ 10 8 2   ◇ A Q 8 4   ♣ 9 6

You do not jump in spades as you would have done if third hand had passed; you simply bid 2 ♠. Again there is some loss of precision; in a competitive situation it would be tactically right to make this bid also with a slightly weaker hand.

THE DOUBLER'S REBID

There has already been some discussion of this subject, because of course you should not double in the first place without some idea of your likely rebid. Remember we are dealing with strong doubles, where you intend in principle to bid again over a forced response from partner. This action may take one of three forms.

1. The raise of responder's suit. The simplest case occurs when partner makes a jump response. His strength is then known within fairly close limits and it is usually easy for the doubler to weigh up the combined hands.

OPPONENT	DOUBLER	OPPONENT	RESPONDER
1 ♡	Double	Pass	2 ♠
Pass	?		

The doubler holds:

♠ A K J 3   ♡ 7 4   ◇ A Q 9 5   ♣ K 10 6

With this hand you raise to 4 ♠—partner has shown at least 9 points and you have 17. With a point or two less you would bid only 3 ♠.

When partner makes a minimum response to the double his range is much wider. Inevitably there is less accuracy.

OPPONENT	DOUBLER	OPPONENT	RESPONDER
1 ♣	Double	Pass	1 ♠
Pass	?		

The doubler holds:

(1) ♠ K J 7 2   ♡ A K 10 6   ◇ K Q 5   ♣ J 3
(2) ♠ A Q 8 2   ♡ K Q 7 3   ◇ 4   ♣ A Q J 5
(3) ♠ A K Q 5   ♡ A 9 3   ◇ A K 10 9 2   ♣ 6

These represent about average hands for a raise to 2 ♠, 3 ♠ and 4 ♠ respectively. With (1) you do not hope to reach game unless partner is super-maximum, but the raise is tactically right, to acquaint partner with the fit and the strength of your hand. With (2) you may expect to make a game if partner is in the upper range; if he is busted you will not make even 3 ♠, but this risk is accepted as the ranges are necessarily so wide. Hand (3) is the very powerful type that you need for a raise to game: The presence of four or more spades in partner's hand, which is all that your partner has promised, will suffice to give some kind of play for this contract.

2. The bid in a new suit. This bid suggests a sound five-card or six-card suit in a strong hand. It tends to deny primary support for the responder's suit—at least when responder's suit is a major. It is not forcing, but since the upper limit is just short of the strength for a direct cue bid, responder may make a forward move with modest values.

OPPONENT	DOUBLER	OPPONENT	RESPONDER
1 ♠	Double	Pass	2 ♣
Pass	2 ♡	Pass	?

Responder holds:

(1) ♠ 9 8 2   ♡ J 8 3   ◇ 10 6   ♣ A 7 5 3 2
(2) ♠ 7 6 4 2   ♡ Q 10 4   ◇ 8 5   ♣ A J 10 6

With (1) responder should muster a raise to 3 ♡. With (2) he is well worth a bid of 4 ♡.

3. The cue bid in the opponent's suit. This trusty old standby may be employed whenever the values for game are present and the best denomination is in doubt. It is often the doubler's best developing move when responder has made a jump bid.

OPPONENT	DOUBLER	OPPONENT	RESPONDER
1 ◊	Double	Pass	2 ♠
Pass	?		

Doubler holds:

♠ K 10 6   ♡ A K J 5   ◊ 7   ♣ A Q 7 3 2

A bid of 3 ♣ would be forcing after partner's encouraging response but would tend to place too much stress on this one feature. The doubler is interested primarily in a rebiddable spade suit, a secondary heart suit or a guard in diamonds, so the best bid is 3 ◊.

The Jump Overcall

The standard meaning of a jump overcall in a suit is to show a rather good hand with at least a sound six-card suit. The high-card strength is well-defined but tends to be influenced by vulnerability, ranging from about the equivalent of a sound opening bid to a maximum, in most cases, of about 16 points.

OPPONENT	OVERCALLER
1 ♣ (or 1 ◊)	2 ♡

The overcaller holds:

♠ J 2   ♡ A Q J 9 6 3   ◊ A Q 4   ♣ 10 6

This represents a sound average hand at equal vulnerability; You would still bid 2 ♡ at unfavorable vulnerability, but you would be uncomfortably aware that you had given your all. Now suppose the opening bid is 1 ♠: not vulnerable, you might bid 3 ♡, vulnerable only 2 ♡.

A jump overcall in a minor suit is likely to be in the upper range. This hand is not too strong for 3 ♣ over an opponent's 1 ♠:

♠ 10 4   ♡ A Q 6   ◇ 8 3   ♣ A K Q J 9 2

Over a 1 ♡ opening you could do worse than to bid 1 NT! One always hopes that a jump overcall in a minor may lead to game in notrump, but if you bid 3 ♣ here, there will be a grave danger that partner may have some values and be unable to move for lack of a heart stopper.

In tournament bridge many players achieve good results by using the jump overcall as a preemptive maneuver on a weak hand with a six-card or longer suit. The standard jump overcall, however, sometimes called the intermediate jump overcall, is a valuable weapon and fits nicely into the overall scheme of things. It frequently gives rise to useful negative inferences, for when your partner doubles for takeout and then shows a one-suited hand, you can place him with a rockcrusher—with anything less he would have made a jump overcall on the first round.

RESPONDING TO A JUMP OVERCALL

Jump overcalls have a well-defined upper limit, so responder does not keep the bidding open, even with useful values, unless he can see hope of game. The overcall shows such a sound suit that responder may raise with as little as two small or a singleton honor. In fact, one of the main advantages of these jump overcalls is that they allow the bidding to proceed smoothly in hands where the partners would otherwise find it difficult to get together. For example:

OPPONENT	OVERCALLER	OPPONENT	RESPONDER
1 ♣	2 ♠	Pass	?

Responder holds:

♠ 8 2   ♡ K Q 8 3   ◊ 9 7 4 2   ♣ A 6 5

The correct bid with this hand is 3 ♠, for the trump support is adequate and it is most unlikely that the overcaller will have a four-card heart suit.

It is not often, after a jump overcall, that the responder wishes to put forward an alternative suit to play in. All the same, it is quite common to bid a new suit, forcing for one round, as an exploratory measure. The bidding goes:

OPPONENT	OVERCALLER	OPPONENT	RESPONDER
1 ♣	2 ♠	Pass	?

Responder holds:

(1) ♠ 5 2   ♡ Q 10 4   ◊ A K J 9 6   ♣ 8 7 4
(2) ♠ 4 3   ♡ Q J 3   ◊ A J 8 3   ♣ K 10 5 4
(3) ♠ K 4   ♡ A K 10 3   ◊ J 10 9 5   ♣ 8 3 2

With (1) responder is worth a bid of 3 ◊, as there are two possibilities of making game: partner may be able to bid 3 NT or jump to 4 ♠. If he simply rebids 3 ♠, responder passes.

With (2) responder bids 2 NT, not forcing, as partner may have no more than the equivalent of opening values and there may be a spade trick to lose. With a solidifying card in partner's suit, responder could just about jump to 3 NT.

Hand (3) is worth a game bid. However, if the overcaller has a club stopper there will probably be nine running tricks in notrump, so the first move should be to bid 3 ♣.

Countering a Preempt

It is part of the natural order of things that the occasion when the opponents are most likely to open with a weak 3-bid or a weak 2-bid is when you happen to hold a powerhouse hand. The standard scheme for competing against these preempts is the same as against one-bids: A direct cue bid is the strongest call, a double is a takeout request, an overcall in notrump is natural, and other overcalls show one-suited hands. All these calls, apart from the cue bid, tend to have a slightly higher upper limit over a preempt than over a one-bid, by reason of the higher level of the bidding. Of more practical importance is that these calls have to be applied with greater flexibility—and frequently with more daring—than over a one-bid.

When there is an opposing preempt, you do not enter only on hands where your own values are such as to provide a secure foundation for this action. To insist on this safety margin would be to permit the enemy preempt to succeed in its objective. Instead, the general approach is to assume that your partner has a fair share of the outstanding points, and to bid accordingly. Bear in mind, too, that there are more points for your partner to hold after an enemy preempt than after a bid of one, for the preempter is very limited in high cards. Suppose there is an opening 3 ♣ on your right and you hold this hand:

♠ Q 4   ♡ Q 7 2   ◇ A K Q J 8 3   ♣ A 10

The safe bid, obviously, is 3 ◇. The *right* bid, at any vulnerability, is 3 NT, despite the spade weakness. If your partner has unwisely chosen this moment to hold a blizzard, you will be mangled. But it is more likely that you will find dummy with 7 or 8 points—a fair share of the outstanding strength—and that these will suffice for game. In effect, one goes by broad probabilities, and one expects sometimes to have to take it on the chin.

To balance these occasional losses you must keep open the possibility of penalizing the preemptive bidder. A double in both second and fourth position is for takeout, so the person who will decide whether to play for penalty is the doubler's partner. Accordingly, in order that he may be enabled to pass the double fairly often, you should not double a preempt unless you are prepared for a pass by partner as well as for a response in any suit.

When your hand is short of quick tricks, and especially when it contains a void in the preempter's suit, try hard for a different call. These are examples where a double, over an opposing 3 ♡, is *not* the best call.

(1) ♠ K Q 10 3   ♡ —   ◇ A K J 10 3   ♣ K Q 9 8
(2) ♠ K Q J 8 7   ♡ 4   ◇ Q J 10 5   ♣ K Q 2

With each of these hands you might double an opening bid of 1 ♡, but at the three-level there is danger of a penalty pass. With (1), therefore, it is better to bid 4 ♡—a slight overbid, but one that can be justified according to the principle of in for a penny, in for a pound. With (2) you simply bid 3 ♠.

The requirement that a double should signify preparedness for any suit does not mean that you should double only with a three-suited pattern. It does mean, however, that you should have somewhere to go if partner responds in your weak suit. Suppose there is an opening 3 ♠ on your right and you hold:

(3) ♠ 8 2   ♡ A 4   ◇ K Q 7 3   ♣ A Q J 5 3
(4) ♠ A 8   ♡ K 10 9 3   ◇ A K Q 8 3   ♣ 9 4
(5) ♠ 7 2   ♡ A K 9 7 4   ◇ K 10 3   ♣ A K 5

With (3) a double would be dangerous, for if partner responded in a four-card heart suit you would be out in the open. (And your partner *will* respond in such a suit if he has one, for from his angle this will represent the best chance of game.) You should therefore overcall with 4 ♣. This also is risky, but it is a risk that cannot be helped.

With (4) again you have a 5-4-2-2 pattern, but because of the rank of the suit it is safe to double. If partner responds 4 ♣ you intend to bid 4 ◇, which will tend to suggest 5-4 in diamonds and hearts. Unless you double you may never discover a 4-4 heart fit.

Hand (5) is an awkward type. Most players would double, intending to pass if partner can bid only 4 ♣ or 4 ◇. Against that, it is likely that the best chance of game is to find partner with three-card support for hearts. If your affairs are in order, therefore, you may decide to continue with 4 ♡, although this can go wrong.

Finally, because you should credit your partner with a share of the outstanding points, it is right to take bold action over an opposing 3 ♡ with this type of hand:

♠ K Q J 10 5   ♡ A 4   ◇ A K J 10   ♣ 9 7

If you are to place partner with 7 or 8 points, then clearly you should bid 4 ♠ rather than 3 ♠. If you do not jump to game with a hand as strong as this, the range of your simple overcalls will be too wide for partner's comfort or discretion.

RESPONDING TO A DOUBLE OR OVERCALL OF A 3-BID

A player who enters over a 3-bid may expect to find some values in the hand opposite—let's say around 7 points. Thus the responder should take minimum action when he has no more than these values. The bidding goes:

OPPONENT	OVERCALLER	OPPONENT	RESPONDER
3 ◇	3 ♡	Pass	?

Both sides are vulnerable and responder holds:

(1) ♠ K 8 3   ♡ 9 6 4   ◇ J 8 2   ♣ K J 7 4
(2) ♠ K 8 6 4   ♡ 10 3   ◇ 7 6 4   ♣ A Q 9 5
(3) ♠ 9 7 5 4   ♡ Q 8 3   ◇ K J 4   ♣ A 10 3

With (1) it is hard to detect that you have any pleasant surprise for partner, and the right action is to pass. Hand (2) is worth a bid, and of course the only sound call is 4 ♡, for you should not bid four-card suits in this situation. Hand (3) presents a choice between 4 ♡ and 3 NT. If you held three little diamonds you would probably pass 3 ♡; therefore, if you are to bid game with your actual hand you should bid 3 NT rather than 4 ♡, as this may be the only way to extract value from the diamond combination.

In responding to a double, again you take minimum action when you have no more than 7 or 8 points. However, when there is a reasonable chance that a fit is present, you may add points for shortness. Your side is vulnerable and the bidding goes:

OPPONENT	PARTNER	OPPONENT	YOU
3 ♡	Double	Pass	?

You hold:

(1) ♠ Q 8 4 3 2   ♡ 9 4 3   ◇ A Q 7   ♣ 10 4
(2) ♠ J 7 3 2   ♡ A 5   ◇ K Q 8 6 4   ♣ 9 2
(3) ♠ 9 8 3   ♡ Q J 9   ◇ J 8 3   ♣ K 7 6 4

With (1) you should be willing to assume that your partner has support for spades. This makes your hand worth 10 points, and you therefore jump to 4 ♠.

With (2) you are still stronger and can afford to cover the chance that partner may not after all have four spades. You bid 4 ♡. If partner responds 4 ♠, you pass; but if he bids 5 ♣ you continue with 5 ◇.

Hand (3) presents an exception to the rule that you do not make a constructive response with less than 9 or 10 points. A bid of 3 NT is of course more sensible than 4 ♣, even though you do not really expect to make it if partner has a minimum double.

Entering at the 4-Level

When the opponents preempt at the level of four-odd, or when the bidding begins with a bid of 1 ♡ or 1 ♠ and there is a preemptive raise to four, some adjustment is needed to the arrangements for introducing a powerhouse hand. The idea now is to double to show all-round strength. The double is not specifically for takeout, but neither does it show strength in the enemy suit. This is the sort of hand with which you would double after 1 ♡-4 ♡ or after an opening 4 ♡:

♠ A K 7   ♡ 5 2   ◇ A 10 8 6   ♣ A K 4 3

The responder passes with a balanced hand, whether weak or moderately strong, and takes out only with quite a long suit. His distribution is almost the sole criterion.

4 NT IN COMPETITION

As a double at the four level is used to show all-round strength, a way has to be found for introducing powerful distributional hands which at a lower level would be dealt with by means of a takeout double or a cue bid in the opponent's suit. The best solution to this problem—or at least the best *partial* solution, for when you have to commence operations at the level of four-odd there are no easy answers—is to use 4 NT as a takeout request.

When the opponents have reached the level of 4 ♠, a bid of 4 NT asks for any one of the other three suits. When the opponents have reached 4 ♡, 4 NT asks for one of the minor suits. To illustrate:

(1)	OPPONENT	OVERCALLER	(2)	OPPONENT	OVERCALLER
	4 ♡	4 NT		4 ♠	4 NT

In (1), where the overcaller is bypassing 4 ♠, 4 NT is a request for the minor suits; it would not be good business for the overcaller to bid 4 NT if interested in a possible spade contract. In (2) the overcaller may have his eye on any of the unbid suits.

This bid of 4 NT is frequently used to introduce a two-suited type of hand. A standard example:

OPPONENT	PARTNER	OPPONENT	YOU
1 ♡	Pass	4 ♡	?

You hold:

♠ A 5   ♡ 7   ◇ K Q J 8 3   ♣ A Q 9 8 2

A bid of 4 NT, asking for a takeout in one of the minor suits, is clearly best. In the next example you have a major-minor two-suiter.

OPPONENT	PARTNER	OPPONENT	YOU
1 ♠	Pass	4 ♠	?

You hold:

♠ 10   ♡ A K J 8 3   ◇ K Q 9 8 4   ♣ K 7

Again you bid 4 NT. If partner responds with 5 ♣, you continue with 5 ◇; partner can then place you with hearts and diamonds.

When a player bids 4 NT over 4 ♠, his partner should normally respond with *the lower-ranking* of two biddable suits, in order to ensure finding a fit at the lowest level.

OPPONENT	YOU	OPPONENT	PARTNER
3 ♠	Pass	4 ♠	4 NT
Pass	?		

You hold:

♠ 8 4   ♡ Q J 10 3   ◇ Q 7 6 4   ♣ 9 5 2

If you bid 5 ♡ and your partner has the minor suits, you may be out of your depth. The correct response is 5 ◇ : then if partner's two-suiter is in clubs and hearts he will bid 5 ♡.

The principle of responding in the lower-ranking suit applies even when this is the shorter suit. You may sometimes have to make quite a startling response to your partner's 4 NT.

OPPONENT	YOU	OPPONENT	PARTNER
3 ♠	Pass	4 ♠	4 NT
Pass	?		

You hold:

♠ 5 2   ♡ 10 3   ◇ A 10 9 4 2   ♣ J 10 6 4

It may seem natural to bid 5 ◇, but your main concern is to ensure that this hand is played in the right suit. As partner may be two-suited, he must be enabled to remove into one of his own suits if your first choice happens to be wrong. The correct bid is therefore 5 ♣.

Quiz on Powerhouse Overcalls

Both sides vulnerable, the player on your right opens 1 ♡. What do you call with each of the following?

(1) ♠ A J 10 7 3 2   ♡ K 5   ◇ A Q 3   ♣ 8 4

(2) ♠ Q J 10 3   ♡ 7   ◇ A K Q J 8 3   ♣ A K
(3) ♠ A K 7   ♡ Q J 5   ◇ A K Q 2   ♣ J 10 3
(4) ♠ 3   ♡ K J 8 3   ◇ K Q 9 2   ♣ A K 4 3
(5) ♠ A Q J 8 7 4 3 2   ♡ 9 2   ◇ 10 4   ♣ A

Neither side vulnerable, the bidding goes:

OPPONENT	PARTNER	OPPONENT	YOU
1 ♠	2 ♠	Pass	?

What is your call with each of the following hands?

(6) ♠ 8 4   ♡ Q 7 6 2   ◇ 6 5   ♣ 10 8 7 4 3
(7) ♠ Q 5 2   ♡ J 10 5 4   ◇ 9 8 2   ♣ 10 7 2
(8) ♠ 10 4   ♡ Q 8 7 4 3 2   ◇ 6   ♣ K J 9 3
(9) ♠ 9 7 4   ♡ K J 3   ◇ 10 9 7 4   ♣ A 10 3
(10) ♠ A Q 8 4   ♡ 8 7 2   ◇ 10 7 2   ♣ J 4 2

Your side is vulnerable and the player on your right opens 3 ♡. What is your call with each of the following?

(11) ♠ 8 5   ♡ K 7 4 3   ◇ K Q 5 2   ♣ A K Q
(12) ♠ A K J 10 3 2   ♡ 4 2   ◇ A 10 9   ♣ A Q
(13) ♠ Q 8 3 2   ♡ 7   ◇ A K Q 10 3   ♣ A J 5
(14) ♠ A Q 10 5   ♡ —   ◇ K Q J 10 9 2   ♣ A K 8
(15) ♠ Q J   ♡ K 4   ◇ K J 6   ♣ A K J 10 6 3

Neither side vulnerable, the bidding goes:

OPPONENT	PARTNER	OPPONENT	YOU
1 ♡	Pass	4 ♡	?

What is your call with each of the following?

(16) ♠ A 8 4   ♡ A 2   ◇ A K 6 2   ♣ K 10 9 4
(17) ♠ 7   ♡ K Q 9 2   ◇ A 10 4 3   ♣ K J 8 3
(18) ♠ A 6   ♡ 4   ◇ A K J 8 3   ♣ Q J 9 8 4
(19) ♠ K Q J 8 4   ♡ 7 4   ◇ A 6   ♣ K Q J 10
(20) ♠ 4   ♡ 7 6 4   ◇ A K 3   ♣ K J 9 8 7 2

Solutions

1. 2 ♠. This hand ranks as a sound jump overcall, for the
   king of hearts will surely be worth a full trick and the
   diamond combination also seems favorably placed; if partner raises to 3 ♠ you should be willing to go on to game.
   The overcall provides a better description than a double.
2. 2 ♡. You have two main chances to make game: (a) partner may have four spades, in which case there is likely to
   be a play for ten tricks, or (b) partner may have a heart
   guard, enabling him to make 3 NT. If partner has a blizzard you may still be able to stop at 4 ◇.
3. Double. With this notrump-type hand, too strong for an
   overcall of 1 NT, the standard procedure is to double and
   bid notrump at the lowest level over a forced response
   from partner.
4. Pass. A double would be unwise with this pattern because
   your high-card values, although above average, may not
   be sufficient if partner insists on a spade contract. In the
   best circles your pattern would also be regarded as a little
   too eccentric for 1 NT. On the whole it is better to await
   developments.
5. 4 ♠. This is just common sense. You would surely be
   unwilling to allow opponents to play this hand anywhere
   below the 5-level, and yet the high-card values do not
   justify a cue bid in the opponent's suit.
6. 3 ♣. No doubt a game is more likely in hearts than in

clubs, but nevertheless you should bid your suits in the natural manner. For one thing, if partner can bid hearts ahead of you, the contract will be played by the right hand.

7. 3 ♡. Your hand contains two possibly valuable features and it is debatable which you should show first. The snag with bidding 2 NT is that partner may be unwilling to mention a four-card heart suit and may raise you to 3 NT. On the other hand, if you bid 3 ♡ and partner does not have four-card support, he may continue with 3 ♠. Now you can bid 3 NT, having hinted that your spade guard is not exactly bombproof.

8. 3 ♡. This is a very promising hand indeed in the circumstances, but all the same it would be wrong to jump to 4 ♡ because partner's cue bid may be based on some kind of minor-suit hand. The first aim after a cue bid is to find a fit. If this fit turns out to be in hearts, or even clubs, you will have some justification for considering slam.

9. 3 ♠. With these values a slam is a strong possibility. Therefore you should not risk a disaster by mentioning this ethereal diamond suit. By offering a responsive cue bid you ensure discovering the most promising trump suit, and at the same time you go some way toward showing your strength.

10. 3 NT. This is a useful way of conveying that you have values, that your spade stopper is cast-iron and that you have no other four-card suit.

11. Pass. Frustrating though it may be, there is very little you can do with this hand—if you were to double your partner would almost certainly bid spades. The hand does not contain the promise of enough tricks for 3 NT.

12. 4 ♠. You should not be willing to risk partner passing a bid of 3 ♠ since you need so little for game. A cue bid of 4 ♡ would be pointless, for there is only one suit you want to play in.

13. Double. This is preferred to 4 ◊, as it may be the only way to reach a spade contract. If partner bids 4 ♣, you continue with 4 ◊.

14. 4 ♡. Here again you should be unwilling to convey the impression of a one-suited hand by overcalling in

diamonds. You hope that partner may respond in spades, but if he does not you are willing to battle it out in 5 ♢.

15. 3 NT. You do not expect to make this contract unless partner can make some appreciable contribution, but it is unlikely that you can make a game elsewhere than in 3 NT.

16. Double. This shows a strong all-round hand. It does not matter that you have only three cards in the unbid major suit, for partner will not remove the double unless he has quite a marked distribution.

17. Pass. You cannot be certain of beating 4 ♡, but your prospects are certainly rosy enough to reject any such enterprise as a bid of 4 NT. A double would not be primarily for penalty, and there would be grave danger of partner removing to 4 ♠.

18. 4 NT. This is a takeout request. You are bypassing 4 ♠, so your partner will realize that you are interested in a minor-suit contract.

19. 4 ♠. A pass would be timid; a double unattractive since the hand is lacking in defensive tricks. The most likely game, after all is 4 ♠.

20. 5 ♣. To say that you are likely to make this contract would be an exaggeration. But your partner is bound to be short of hearts, and has not preempted in spades, so you may be fortunate enough to find at least some ruffing values in his hand.

10

The Precision 1 ♣

♠ ♡ ◇ ♣

The Precision 1 ♣ Opening—Rebids After a Negative Response—Positive Responses to 1 ♣—The "Unusual Positive"—When Opponents Intervene Over 1 ♣

In general there is virtue in simple methods that use no more bids than are necessary. This, however, should not blind us to the possibility that powerhouse hands, because of the realities of the scoring table, merit special treatment. Slam bonuses—and slam failures—exert a disproportionate influence on results. There is no question that any system which aims to excel in slam bidding must be founded on the idea of making as many exploratory bids as possible below the level of game.

This leads logically to the suggestion that the artificial forcing opening should be not 2 ♣ but 1 ♣, and that the strength required for this opening should be reduced so that it may cater to a greater number of hands.

In the early days of contract bridge there were many systems where an opening 1 ♣ was artificial, usually with a conventional response of 1 ◇ to show weakness. Why none of these caught on is an interesting question. But the important thing now is that many tournament players, recognizing the success of Italian teams using an artificial 1 ♣ in world events, have turned to modern systems based on this principle. The most popular of these is the Precision System developed by C. C. Wei of New York; the author is grateful for his assistance in the organization of this chapter. As this system has proved so successful, and as so much highpowered thought has gone in and continues to go into its development, the serious player will wish to consider whether he too should turn to Precision so that he can benefit from advances made by leading players.

The basis of the Precision System is easily described:

Forcing 1 ♣ opening with 16 high-card points or more. Natural responses in five-card suits except for 1 ◇ to show fewer than 8 points.

Five-card major-suit openings with limit raises and forcing 1 NT responses.

From 13 to 15 high-card points for 1 NT opening.

Natural, non-forcing 2 ♣ opening with 11-15 high-card points. This is primarily a consequence of not being able to open these hands with 1 ♣.

Weak Two's in the major suits.

The reader may note that apart from the 1 ♣ opening the main structure of the system consists of well-tried methods that are famil- iar to most Standard players. We will not dwell upon these features, as the purpose here is to afford the Standard player a glimpse of the 1 ♣ convention at work, so that he may observe the advantage of this method of dealing with powerhouse hands and perhaps incorpo- rate it into his normal methods for the purpose of testing it further. There are, of course, a number of excellent books on the complete Precision System.

The Precision 1 ♣ Opening

Almost all hands of 16 or more high-card points are opened with 1 ♣, regardless of distribution. The 1 ♣ opening is forcing for one round. Balanced hands of 22 or 23 points are an exception and are opened with 2 NT.

Distributional points are not counted in Precision except in one situation: when raising partner's suit. In this case you add five points for a void, three for a singleton and one for a doubleton. In all other situations you count honor points only. Of course you may take account of whether your points are working well or not—just as you would in any system—but this applies to the later rounds of bidding. You do not open 1 ♣ with less than 16 points unless you have exceptional distribution such as:

♠ A Q J 10 8 5 4   ♡ —   ◇ 10 6   ♣ A K J 4

With this hand you may open 1 ♣ and still hope to keep matters under control since your suit is self-sufficient. In the same way you might decide *not* to open 1 ♣ with an unattractive 16 points if these included, say, the bare Q-J of a suit. These exceptions are rare, however. In general you stick closely to the 16-point standard. This is especially so with two-suited hands.

♠ K Q J 7 2   ♡ 4   ◇ A J 9 6 3   ♣ A 2

Precision bidders have found that to open 1 ♣ with this type of hand and then bid two suits is apt to give an exaggerated impression of strength. Here you would open 1 ♠, showing a five-card suit. Now you can bid your hand quite powerfully, showing diamonds on the next round, for partner will know that you can have no more than 15 points.

Rebids After a Negative Response

With 0-7 points the responder makes the negative bid of 1 ◇. This warns opener that responder does not undertake to bid again unless opener continues with another forcing bid. The 1 ◇ response is artificial, of course, saying nothing about responder's diamond holding.

After 1 ♣-1 ◇ the opener's next moves follow a simple but very descriptive scheme. With no five-card suit, he normally rebids in notrump: 1 NT shows 16-18 points, 2 NT shows 19-21 points, 3 NT shows 24-26 points. Hands of 22 or 23 points are opened with

2 NT, so this scheme takes very good care of all balanced openings.

With an unbalanced hand the opener, after 1 ♣-1 ◇, continues with either a jump bid in a suit or a simple bid in a suit, according to the strength of his hand.

THE JUMP REBID IN A SUIT AFTER 1 ♣-1 ◇

This bid is forcing to at least the 3-level and is based on at least a strong five-card suit. Opener is likely to have at least 22 points, or an exceptionally powerful distributional hand. There is no upper limit of strength. In other words, this sequence shows the type of hand that might be opened with 2 ♣ or a Forcing Two in Standard methods.

OPENER	RESPONDER
1 ♣	1 ◇
2 ♠	

The following would be typical hands for this bidding sequence:

(1) ♠ A Q J 10 8   ♡ K Q 10 4   ◇ A Q 5   ♣ A
(2) ♠ A K Q J 7 4 3   ♡ A Q J   ◇ 4   ♣ Q 7

It is unnecessary for opener to make a jump rebid with any appreciably weaker hand, for he has already shown at least 16 points by opening with 1 ♣. His partner, therefore, will keep the bidding open with quite slender values over a simple rebid.

After a jump rebid in a suit, responder is obliged to bid once more. The broad idea now is that he raises with three-card support for this suit, proceeding as follows:

0-3 points .... single raise
4-7 points .... double raise

Lacking three-card support for opener's suit, responder's next move depends on his strength. With a worthless hand he may bid notrump, which has the meaning of a double negative. With any useful suit, however, he avoids this bid; having already limited his hand to a maximum of 7 points, he may make a constructive move on very little.

This is how you would proceed with different types of responding hands:

OPENER	RESPONDER
1 ♣	1 ◇
2 ♡	?

Responder holds:

(1) ♠ 5 4   ♡ 9 7 6   ◇ 8 6 3 2   ♣ Q J 8 4
(2) ♠ K J 10 3   ♡ 6   ◇ 9 8 5 4   ♣ 10 7 3 2
(3) ♠ 10 8 2   ♡ 6 3   ◇ 9 7 4 3   ♣ J 5 3 2
(4) ♠ K J 3   ♡ 10 8 7   ◇ Q 9 8 4   ♣ 7 5 2

With (1) you would raise to 3 ♡; this is in no sense an overbid as your hand contains several features that may help your partner. With (2) you are also worth a constructive move, in this case 2 ♠. Here, however, you intend to pass if partner's next bid is 3 ♡.

Hand (3) contains no useful feature so you bid 2 NT, a double negative, again intending to pass if partner rebids 3 ♡. Hand (4) is treated as a maximum, and with three-card support you jump to 4 ♡.

THE SIMPLE REBID IN A SUIT AFTER 1 ♣-1 ◇

A simple rebid in a suit by opener after 1 ♣-1 ◇ shows an unbalanced hand in the range of 16-21 points; to be more accurate, it shows a hand of this strength which is unsuitable for a bid in notrump. Responder may have as many as 7 points, so game is still a possibility.

Some examples follow of the responder's action after 1 ♣-1 ◇-1 ♡. Responder holds:

♠ K 8 7 4 2   ♡ 6 4   ◇ J 8 3 2   ♣ 7 5

Here you bid 1 ♠. You have only four points, but as you have a useful major suit there is still a chance of game.

♠ J 6 5   ♡ 7 6 4   ◇ K 8 5 4   ♣ 9 5 2

With this hand you pass. There cannot be more than 25 points in the two hands and there is no strong fit. This is about the strongest hand on which you would pass; with one point more you would bid 1 NT.

♠ Q 9 4   ♡ J 5   ◇ Q J 8 6 4   ♣ 10 7 2

This hand is worth a bid of 2 ◇, which shows a five-card suit and 5-7 points. The 2-level bid is encouraging but not forcing.

♠ 8 2   ♡ 10 7 6 4   ◇ 9 6 5 4   ♣ K 4 2

With this hand you raise to 2 ♡, partly because game is not impossible but also because it is tactically right to show three-card or longer support for opener's suit unless your hand is a complete write-off. This single raise suggests 2-4 points; a double raise shows 5-7 points with four-card support. In all these examples it is easy to see how much more accurate the exchanges are than in Standard methods.

When the opener has a powerful two-suited hand, this style of bidding leaves him very comfortably placed. After 1 ♣-1 ◇ he should not feel under any pressure to force with borderline values, as he will usually have a chance to show the second suit. For example:

♠ A Q 10 8 4   ♡ A Q J 7 5   ◇ J   ♣ A 9

With this hand opener rebids only 1 ♠. Responder may raise with very little, or may bid 1 NT, providing opener with a chance to show hearts. The responder may sometimes make a strong game invitational bid after his 1 ◇ negative, holding good trump support and a near-maximum, such as:

OPENER	RESPONDER
♠ A Q 8 5 2	♠ K 10 6 4
♡ A K 6 3	♡ 8 4
◇ K J 9	◇ 7 5 2
♣ 4	♣ A 9 6 3

OPENER	RESPONDER
1 ♣	1 ◇
1 ♠	3 ♠
4 ♠	Pass

Responder lacks the 8 high-card points needed for a positive response on the first round, but in support of spades his hand increases to 8 points and these include prime values. His jump raise is not absolutely forcing, and if opener held a bare 16 points and lacked top-card controls he might pass.

Positive Responses to 1 ♣

We come now to the important class of hands where the responder has 8 or more points and shows this strength by a positive response: either a simple suit bid with a five-card or longer suit, or a bid in notrump. With these hands the advantages of low-level exploration are potentially greatest.

NOTRUMP RESPONSES TO 1 ♣

A responder who has 8 or more points and no five-card suit responds in notrump according to this schedule:

With 8-13 points .... 1 NT
With 14 or more points .... 2 NT

When the bidding begins with 1 ♣-1 NT, the opener's rebids. follow a very predictable pattern: 2 ♣ at this point is Stayman, asking the responder to name a four-card major suit or to bid 2 ◇. With 8-10 high-card points responder uses customary Stayman responses: 2 ◇ shows no four-card major; 2 ♠ or 2 ♡ shows a four-card suit. With 11-13 high-card points, responder postpones the Stayman response, bidding 2 NT to show values with any balanced hand, whereupon 3 ♣ by opener is a request for responder to show a four-card major suit.

A raise from 1 NT to 2 NT shows a minimum balanced opening and is not forcing:

OPENER	RESPONDER
1 ♣	1 NT
2 NT	

Opener is showing 16 or 17 points and the responder may pass with 8, but in practice will rarely do so.

A simple bid in a new suit by opener, other than 2 ♣, is natural, showing at least five cards, and has the meaning of an asking bid.

OPENER	RESPONDER
1 ♣	1 NT
2 ◇ (2 ♡, 2 ♠)	

Opener's rebid in this sequence is forcing to game, for after the 1 NT response it is assumed that there cannot be a bad misfit. Partner rebids conventionally by steps to show support and number of controls—ace is 2, king is 1.

Steps	Suit Support	Total Controls
1	Poor (J-x-x or less)	Few (3 or less)
2	Poor	Good (4 or more)
3	Good (Q-x-x or better)	Few (3 or less)
4	Good	Good
5	Four small cards	Good

To illustrate the accuracy of this mechanism, here is how support-asking bids, followed by natural bidding, work after a positive response of 1 NT.

OPENER	RESPONDER
♠ 9	♠ K 7 3 2
♡ A K Q 8 4	♡ J 10 7 2
◇ A K 9 8 5 4	◇ Q J 3
♣ 8	♣ A 7

OPENER	RESPONDER
1 ♣	1 NT (a)
2 ◇ (b)	2 NT (c)
3 ♡ (d)	4 ♡ (e)
4 NT (f)	5 ◇ (g)
6 ♡	Pass

(a) 8-13 high-card points; balanced hand
(b) Support-asking in diamonds
(c) Good support but fewer than four controls
(d) Natural; at least a four-card suit
(e) Natural; at least four-card support
(f) Blackwood
(g) One ace

Notice that the support-asking bid does not necessarily set the trump suit.

After a 2 NT response (14 or more high-card points) to a 1 ♣ opening, opener may bid 3 ♣ as a conventional Stayman inquiry or, by arrangement, as a request to responder to show his four-card suits up the line. With 3-3-3-4, responder rebids 3 NT showing that his only four-card suit is clubs.

SUIT RESPONSES TO 1 ♣

A positive response of 1 ♡, 1 ♠, 2 ♣ or 2 ◇ shows a five-card or longer suit and 8 or more high-card points. It is forcing, but not necessarily to game; when the later bidding shows clear signs of a misfit, it is possible to play at 2 NT or three of a suit. This again is an area where Precision pairs find it easier to stop at a makable contract than Standard bidders.

The opener's rebids follow a natural pattern. With a balanced hand he makes a rebid in notrump. With a five-card or longer suit he bids this suit at the minimum level (a support asking bid), and from then the bidding proceeds along commonsense lines.

OPENER	RESPONDER
♠ A Q J 9 5	♠ K 7 6 2
♡ A K 4	♡ —
◇ A K 9 4	◇ Q 7 6 3 2
♣ 9	♣ A Q 3 2

OPENER	RESPONDER
1 ♣	2 ◇
2 ♠	4 ♡ (Splinter)
5 ◇ (Cue)	6 ♣ (Cue)
7 NT	Pass

Here, Precision bidding can hardly fail to reach the grand slam—in notrump, spades or diamonds. Responder's 4 ♡ is recognizable as a splinter because it bypasses the conventional support-asking responses: the splinter shows good spade support, singleton or void in the heart suit and slam interest. Looking at two solid five-card suits and the ace-king of hearts, when responder bids 6 ♣ to show the ♣ ace, opener knows exactly where to go!

An attractive and very logical feature of Precision comes into operation when the opener gives a direct raise of his partner's suit with three-card support. In this case the scheme is:

With a minimum opening hand, raise straight to game. This is the opposite of the Standard procedure. It is logical in this forcing situation, for with such a hand slam is least likely to be there. Responder, of course, is not barred from going on with a very powerful hand.

With 19-21 points, including support points (5, 3, 1 for void, singleton, doubleton), raise to the 3-level. This tells partner to take over with a good hand and slam aspirations.

With 22 points upwards, make a single raise. Now you have maximum space for exploring a slam. This raise is in fact a *trump-asking bid.* (Formerly "optional," this is now standard, except in Simplified Precision.) Responder's next bid will show how good his suit is according to the "step" system. Each step is the lowest possible subsequent bid, including notrump. Thus:

Suit Length	No. of Top Honors (A-K-Q)	Steps
5 or more cards	0	1
5 cards	1	2
5 cards	2	3
6 or more cards	1	4
6 or more cards	2	5
5 or more cards	3	6

To illustrate:

OPENER	RESPONDER
1 ♣	1 ♠
2 ♠ (Asking bid)	?

How should responder proceed with the following hands:

(1) ♠ A Q 7 6 2   ♡ 10 4 2   ◇ 7 6 3   ♣ K 6
(2) ♠ K 10 9 6 3 2   ♡ A Q 8   ◇ 5 4   ♣ 10 7

With (1) the responder's next bid is 3 ◇. This three-step response shows a five-card suit and two of the three top honors. With (2) he bids 3 ♡, showing a six-card suit with one top honor.

After a trump-asking bid in responder's suit and the step response, a new suit by opener is a control-asking bid. Responder again shows his holding in the asked suit by "steps."

Control in the Asked Suit	*Steps*
No control (3 low cards)	1
Third-round control (doubleton or Q)	2
Second-round control (singleton or K)	3
First-round control (void or A)	4
First- and second-round control (A-K or A-Q)	5

If a control-asking bid is made at the 5-level, the responses are reduced to three steps:

No control or third-round control	1
Second-round control	2
First-round control	3

After a control-asking bid by opener and the step response, a bid of a new suit by opener is also a control-asking bid; responder makes the same step response as above. A repeat bid of the same asked suit by opener is a request for clarification of the quality of control in the asked suit:

Step Response to Control-Asking Bid

					Steps for Clarifying Bid
1 step	2 steps	3 steps	4 steps	5 steps	
3 low	doubleton	singleton	void	A-Q	1
4 low	Q	K	A	A-K	2

Let's have a look at how this system works:

OPENER		RESPONDER	
♠	A Q 8 4	♠	K 10 7 5 2
♡	Q 7 4 2	♡	A K
◇	A	◇	10 7 6 2
♣	A K Q 6	♣	8 4

OPENER	RESPONDER
1 ♣	1 ♠
2 ♠	3 ♣
3 ♡	4 ♡
7 ♠	Pass

With 10 high-card points and a five-card spade suit, responder has a positive response. Opener has 21 high-card points and an extremely good spade fit. He therefore takes the captaincy and settles the trump suit by bidding 2 ♠. At the same time he asks for information about his partner's suit. When responder bids 3 ♣ he has gone up by two steps, showing one high honor in spades and a five-card suit. Opener can see that the trump suit should be good enough for slam, but he is not certain that the hearts are safe. Thus he asks in that suit by bidding 3 ♡. Responder goes up five steps and bids 4 ♡, showing two honors in the suit. With this perfect fit it would be odd indeed if the grand slam were not on, so opener ends the auction by bidding 7 ♠.

OPENER	RESPONDER
♠ A K 2	♠ Q 9 7
♡ K 6 5 3	♡ J 9 7 4 2
◇ 9	◇ K Q 8 6
♣ A K Q 8 4	♣ 10

OPENER	RESPONDER
1 ♣	1 ♡
2 ♡	2 ♠
4 ♡	Pass

When responder can make a positive response to 1 ♣, opener has a fine hand in support of hearts. He starts his investigations by bidding 2 ♡, asking how strong his partner's trumps are. Responder denies a top honor by bidding only one step. Opener knows at once that both the ♡ ace and ♡ queen are missing. He therefore contents himself with bidding 4 ♡.

THE JUMP-SHIFT REBID BY OPENER

Precision players aim to extract every conceivable advantage, and there is one more specialized rebid by opener after a positive response to 1 ♣. This is a jump shift. A single jump in a new suit shows 19 or more points *and a solid six-card or longer suit* —usually A-K-Q-10-x-x at least. For example:

OPENER	RESPONDER
1 ♣	1 ♠
3 ♡	

This jump shift sets the trump suit. A bid in a new suit by the responder now will be a cue bid, showing a feature and extra values. With a minimum hand responder raises the suit or bids notrump.

RESPONDER'S ACTION ON THE SECOND ROUND

An important concept in Precision—when not playing the support-asking bid—is that the responder, after having given a positive response, should consider whether his hand is "minimum" or "maximum" and should show this with his next bid.

> A *maximum positive response* consists of 11 points or more with at least four controls (ace = two controls, king = one control).

> A *minimum positive response* consists of any hand with 8-10 points and any stronger hand that has only three or fewer controls.

With a minimum positive response the responder takes minimum action on the second round: He rebids notrump at the lowest level, gives a single raise of opener's suit with three-card or longer support, or rebids his own suit at the lowest level.

With a maximum positive response he makes a strong bid on the second round: a jump rebid in notrump, a jump raise of opener's suit, a jump rebid in a sound six-card suit, or a jump bid in a new four-card suit (which should be at least as good as K-Q-x-x). In these examples you hold the responding hand:

OPENER	RESPONDER
1 ♣	1 ♡
1 ♠	?

Responder holds:

♠ K 6 2   ♡ A J 7 5 4   ◇ 9 3   ♣ K 10 4 .

Here you raise to 3 ♠. This hand is perhaps not as distributional as it would be in a comparable Standard sequence, but this does not matter. The big thing is that you are distinguishing your

values, and your partner will not bank on more than three-card
support for spades, for he has shown a five-card suit. Note that this
hand counts as 12 points in support of spades, because you may add
a point for a doubleton when raising partner's suit.

	OPENER	RESPONDER
	1 ♣	1 ♠
	2 ♡	?

Responder holds:

♠ K Q 9 7 3   ♡ J 6   ◇ K 9 8   ♣ Q J 2

Here you bid simply 2 NT, for although you have 12 points
you do not have the four controls needed for a jump bid at this point.

STOPPING SHORT OF GAME AFTER
A POSITIVE RESPONSE TO 1 ♣

It was remarked earlier that Precision players sometimes gain
by staying out of unmakable games that would be reached by Standard players. This is because with the bidding level kept lower,
evidence of a misfit tends to emerge while there is still time to do
something about it. In such case the bidding may stop at 2 NT or
three of a suit.

In the next example there are 25 high-card points in the two
hands. Most Standard pairs would find it hard to stay out of 3 NT or
four of a major.

OPENER		RESPONDER	
♠	A 8	♠	K 10 7 6 3
♡	Q J	♡	A 8 6 5 4
◇	A 8 4 2	◇	J 6
♣	A Q 8 4 3	♣	10

A Precision pair might bid these hands as follows:

OPENER	RESPONDER
1 ♣	1 ♠
2 ♣	2 ♡
2 NT	3 ♡
3 ♠	Pass

Note that the responder, on the fourth round, is not under the slightest pressure to bid game; he has shown his hand perfectly and has nothing in reserve. If game were a reasonable contract, the opener would surely have bid 4 ♠ rather than three.

On the second round the opener might well have elected to bid 2 ♠ rather than 2 NT. The final contract should still be the same, for responder would bid 3 ♠ and opener should pass.

The principle that misfit hands may be dropped at 2 NT or three of a suit does not apply when responder's first bid is in a minor suit. When the bidding starts in that way, it is hard to identify a misfit below the level of 3 NT. Most Precision players have therefore found it convenient to arrange that after 1 ♣-2 ♣ or 1 ♣-2 ◇, the bidding may not stop below 3 NT or four of a minor suit.

THE "UNUSUAL POSITIVE"

There is one type of hand that is not catered for in the scheme of positive responses to the 1 ♣ opening. With a balanced hand you bid notrump, and with an unbalanced hand you respond in a five-card suit. But suppose you have positive values with a 4-4-4-1 distribution? Partner opens 1 ♣ and you hold:

♠ Q J 9 2   ♡ 6   ◇ K 9 8 3   ♣ A 8 6 5

To bid notrump with this hand would be most misleading, and you may not bid 1 ♠ with only a four-card suit. You seem to be stymied, yet the system makes a very neat provision for this, and it can in fact be described even more precisely than other hands. Responder makes a jump bid *in his singleton suit!*

Opener will know that when he hears this jump bid, the responder has a positive three-suited hand.

OPENER	RESPONDER
1 ♣	2 ♠

This is an "Unusual Positive" sequence. Responder is showing a hand with 8 points or more and precisely four hearts, four diamonds and four clubs.

OPENER	RESPONDER
♠ A J 8 6	♠ K Q 9 4
♡ 8 5 3	♡ 7
◇ A Q 9	◇ K 10 4 2
♣ A Q 10	♣ K 7 5 2

OPENER	RESPONDER
1 ♣	2 ♡ (a)
2 ♠ (b)	3 ♣ (c)
3 ◇ (d)	3 ♠ (e)
4 ♣ (f)	4 ◇ (g)
6 ♠ (h)	Pass

(a) Unusual positive—8 or more high-card points, 4-4-4-1 distribution with a singleton heart.

(b) Confirms spades as the agreed trump suit.

(c) Responder has good spade support and values in excess of the 8 high-card points needed for a positive response, so he cue-bids his club feature.

(d) Opener has only 17 high-card points—*but* he knows that none of his high cards are wasted opposite responder's known heart singleton. He cooperates in the search for slam by cue-bidding his diamond feature.

(e) Not strong enough for another cue bid at this point.

(f) Club feature. If opener's clubs and hearts were switched, he would sign off in 4 ♠ because some of his honors would be wasted.

(g) Diamond feature.

(h) Responder is known to have club and diamond features, a singleton heart and extra values, so the small slam must be an excellent bet.

Thus the unusual positive produces an unusually excellent result: a virtually cold small slam reached on a combined holding of 28 high-card points!

When Opponents Intervene Over 1 ♣

Many players have the idea that it must be easy to interfere with the machinery of the Precision 1 ♣ opening, but this is not the case. The fact that the opener has already shown a strong hand is a great advantage and affords a sound foundation for partnership action. This usually outweighs the fact that the opener has not shown his real suit.

It was noted in Chapter 7 that the responder has more calls at his disposal in a contested auction than if there had been no intervention. The Precision scheme of defense exploits this very well. The method of dealing with overcalls through 2 ♠ is as follows:

OPENER	OPPONENT	RESPONDER	OPPONENT
1 ♣	1 ♠	?	

Responder's action with 0-8 points

0-4 points..................... ....Pass
5-8 points, no 5-card suit, no stopper ....Negative double
5-8 points, 5-card suit ....Bid this suit
6-8 points, 1 stopper ....Minimum NT bid

Responder's action with 9 points or more

No 5-card suit, no stopper but at least second-round control in
opponent's suit ....Cue-bid opponent's suit.
No 5-card suit, no stopper, no control ....Negative double
         (cue-bid opponent's suit at next turn)
Good 5-card or longer suit............................Negative double
         (show suit at next turn: forcing to game)
9-11 points, at least one stopper ....Jump to 2 NT
12-14 points, at least one stopper ....Double jump to 3 NT

In the case of overcalls at the level of 2 NT or higher, it is
better for the responder to proceed naturally: A double is for penalty, a bid in a new suit is unlimited and forcing if below game, and
3 NT is natural with, of course, a stopper in the opponent's suit.
With game-going values, at least 9 or 10 points and no five-card
suit, responder may cue-bid the suit of the overcall.

When second hand doubles 1 ♣ the recommended procedure
is to pass with 0-4 points and to give the usual 1 ◇ negative with
5-7 points. All positive responses over a double retain their normal
meaning, but there is now one more additional call: A redouble
shows positive values with four cards in both major suits.

Here is an example from World Championship play, where the
Republic of China team that first brought Precision international
acclaim used the opportunity for an extra bid provided by interference bidding after a 1 ♣ opening.

West dealer
Vul: 0

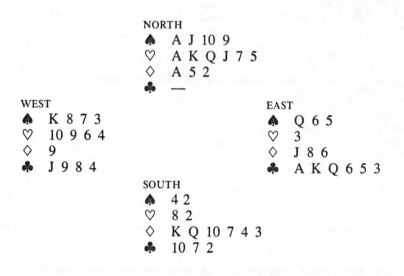

NORTH
♠ A J 10 9
♡ A K Q J 7 5
♢ A 5 2
♣ —

WEST
♠ K 8 7 3
♡ 10 9 6 4
♢ 9
♣ J 9 8 4

EAST
♠ Q 6 5
♡ 3
♢ J 8 6
♣ A K Q 6 5 3

SOUTH
♠ 4 2
♡ 8 2
♢ K Q 10 7 4 3
♣ 10 7 2

WEST (Szvarc)	NORTH (C.S. Shen)	EAST (Boulenger)	SOUTH (F. Huang)
Pass	1 ♣	2 ♣	2 ♢
3 ♣	4 ♣	Pass	4 ♢
Pass	5 ♣	Pass	6 ♢
Pass	7 ♢	Pass	Pass
Pass			

West led the four of clubs.

After the overcall South was able to bid diamonds freely (5-8 high-card points and at least a five-card suit). Two subsequent cue bids by North convinced South that the sixth card in a strong suit was worth a jump to 6 ♢. North could therefore count 13 tricks: six diamonds, six hearts and the ace of spades, not counting a possible ruff in clubs.

When France held the North-South hands, North opened with 2 ♣ and South did not have the required strength for a free bid over East's 3 ♣ overcall. Unable to judge the solidity of the trump suit, North stopped at 6 ◊ ; Taiwan gained 12 International Match Points.

So if you use the Precision Club on your powerhouse hands, be sure to learn what added bids are at your command when the opponents butt in. Used in this way, the opponents' bids can be turned to your advantage.